MAKE MONEY

IN

ABANDONED PROPERTIES

MAKE MONEY

IN

ABANDONED PROPERTIES

How to Identify and Buy Vacant Properties and Make a Huge Profit

CHANTAL HOWELL CAREY
BILL CAREY

WILEY

John Wiley & Sons, Inc.

Published by John Wiley & Sons, Inc., Hoboken, New Jersey.
Published simultaneously in Canada.

For general information on our other products and services or for technical support, please contact our Customer Care Department within the United States at (800) 762-2974, outside the United States at (317) 572-3993 or fax (317) 572-4002.

Wiley also publishes its books in a variety of electronic formats. Some content that appears in print may not be available in electronic books. For more information about Wiley products, visit our web site at www.wiley.com.

Library of Congress Cataloging-in-Publication Data:
Howell Carey, Chantal.
    Make money in abandoned properties: how to identify and buy vacant properties and make a huge profit / Chantal Howell Carey, Bill Carey.
    p. cm.
Includes index.
ISBN-13: 978-0-471-78673-3 (cloth)
ISBN-10: 0-471-78673-X (cloth)
    1. Real estate investment—United States. 2. Abandonment of property—United States. 3. Real property—Purchasing—United States. I. Carey, Bill, 1951-   II. Title.
HD255.H657   2006
332.6324—dc22   2006009976

Printed in the United States of America.

10 9 8 7 6 5 4 3 2 1

With love to all our family, friends, and dedicated students!
May you always have more blessings than you need!

CONTENTS

PREFACE

The abandoned-property market is an undiscovered gold mine. Every neighborhood in every city or town has abandoned properties. The clues can be as obvious as the foot-high grass and the overgrown landscaping or as subtle as an accumulation of flyers on the front door and several days of newspapers in the driveway.

Owners abandon their property for three main reasons. The number-one reason is financial. Typically, a job loss leads to a downward financial spiral. A job transfer can also cause financial hardship. There may be an injury or illness in the family that creates a huge money problem. Rather than face the embarrassment of a foreclosure and forcible eviction, the owners abandon their property and move on.

The second reason owners abandon their property is death or divorce. Besides the financial burden, it may become too unbearable psychologically or emotionally for the surviving or remaining owner to stay in the property.

The third reason owners abandon their property is because the property becomes uninhabitable. There may be a major environmental problem that affects an entire neighborhood. Or one of the owners or family members develops an allergic reaction to the property itself. Over the next five years, people becoming allergic to their homes is going to develop into a major health problem recognized by the general public.

Finally, a weather-related catastrophe or a fire can also make a property uninhabitable. Property owners in Texas and the Gulf Coast states are still reeling from the impact of Hurricanes Rita and Katrina. If the owners are uninsured, they may elect to abandon the property rather than rebuild.

Whatever the reasons for the owners to abandon their property, there is an opportunity for the savvy investor to

make money. We will show you how to find abandoned properties and locate the owners by being observant and doing
some investigating. We will then teach you how to negotiate
with the owners to get the title to the property.

It has been our experience that when you present the
owners a solution to their unresolved property problem,
the owners will take it. We tell the owners that even though
they have abandoned their property, ultimately, if they have
a loan on the property, their lender will foreclose. By making a
deal with us, the owner will avoid a foreclosure.

We tell owners who have no loans on their property that
the local taxing authority will foreclose on their property for
back property taxes even though the owners have abandoned
the property. By making a deal with us, the property-tax foreclosure will be avoided.

Make Money in Abandoned Properties is the first and only
book of its kind. We have found no books on the market that
deal with investing in abandoned properties. The purpose of this
book is to inform you about the existence of the abandoned-
property market and show you how you can easily get involved
with this undiscovered real estate investment and quickly make
money finding and buying abandoned property.

This book is not about foreclosures, tax liens, or flipping.
However, we will discuss foreclosures, tax liens, and flipping
in the appropriate chapters as they relate to finding and buying abandoned property.

This book will show you how to systematically find abandoned property using the 10 clues we use to identify abandoned property. We will teach you five ways to locate the
owners who have abandoned their property. We will then
present the five requirements that must be included in your
foolproof offer.

We will show you how to present your offer and negotiate with the owners so the owners will accept your offer or
make a counteroffer. Next, we will teach you the four ways to
obtain financing to hold or rehab the property. We will also
present creative financing ideas to help close the deal.

We will provide you the information to negotiate with
an abandoned-property owner in foreclosure. We will tell

you how to maximize your profit potential in the property by using a long-term wealth-building or quick-cash strategy. You may decide to assign your accepted contract for quick cash. You may decide to rehab and hold the property for rental income for long-term wealth building.

Finally, we will present how to find motivated partners to get the money to complete your abandoned-property deal. We will close the book with information on what to do if the owner files for bankruptcy protection and what paperwork is necessary to close the transaction.

Abandoned Property = Make Money

Sometimes abandoned property just falls into your lap. We were driving through a neighborhood close to where we live. We saw a property with a for-sale-by-owner sign in the front yard. We stopped and began to notice the telltale signs of an abandoned property.

The landscaping was overgrown with weeds. The grass needed to be watered and mowed. Trash had blown into the flower beds. We went to the front door to ring the bell. There was a major pile of bird droppings on the stoop. No one answered the door. We looked in the windows and saw no furniture. The property was vacant.

We called the number on the for-sale-by-owner sign. We made an appointment with the owners to see the property. When the owners arrived, we discovered they had moved out of the property six months ago. They had tried to rent the property but had been unsuccessful.

The owners were too busy at their work and lived too far away to spend the necessary time to successfully market their property. They were desperate for a solution. They were on the verge of walking away from the property completely. This was an abandoned property waiting to happen!

We determined the property was worth $195,000 to $205,000, depending on its condition. The owners had a mortgage of $157,000. They were trying to sell the property for

$175,000. The owners told us that if they could get $5,000 cash, they would sell us the property! This deal was starting to look pretty good.

Property Value	$200,000
Mortgage	$157,000
Property Equity	$43,000

For $5,000 we would have a $43,000 equity position in the property! However, with abandoned property you must investigate a bit farther. We told the owners we were interested in buying their property. We wanted to do some research before we made them an offer.

We discovered that the loan payments were current and were $1,200 per month. The property taxes were current, but six months of property taxes were accumulated and amounted to $2,500. We inspected the property and realized we would have to replace the carpeting. This would cost $4,000.

We went back to the owners and said we would buy their property under the following conditions. We would give them their requested $5,000. If we were going to give them $5,000, however, we wanted them to compensate us $4,000 for the carpeting, $2,500 for the six months of property taxes that were their responsibility, and $3,600 for the next three mortgage payments.

We explained to the owners that they would be responsible for three mortgage payments if we had a 90-day closing. If they agreed to our offer, we would close in three days. How did the deal look now?

Owner Pays Carpeting	$4,000
Owner Pays Taxes	$2,500
Owner Pays Three Monthly Payments	$3,600
Total	$10,100
Buyer Credits Owner	$5,000
Buyer Receives at Closing	$5,100

Why did the owners agree to our offer? Because they had already abandoned the property. They had moved out. They

wanted to be free of the property. It was just a matter of a relatively short period of time before they would have stopped
making the mortgage payments and gone into foreclosure.
The owners paid us $5,100 to make their abandoned property
problem go away.

   We now had a $43,000 equity position and $5,100 cash
in our pockets. Now you know why we say you can make
money finding and buying abandoned property! With *Make
Money in Abandoned Properties,* you will have all the knowledge and information to be able to successfully do this for
yourself. Good reading and successful investing.

INTRODUCTION

Over the years, we have traveled throughout the country teaching real estate, financial, motivational, and interpersonal skills seminars to our students. We are always striving to be on the leading edge.

Regarding real estate, we have taught everything from buying and selling it creatively as an individual or an investor to core classes for licensing and passing real estate broker's exams. Just about anything you can think of related to real estate, we have taught to someone somewhere!

With a new market comes new ideas. We have distilled the knowledge and experience we have gained from buying and selling real estate for ourselves and our clients and from helping our students over the last three decades.

Make Money in Abandoned Properties is the tenth real estate book we have written. Our first book, *How to Sell Your Home Without a Broker* (2004), is in its fourth edition. Robert J. Bruss, a nationally syndicated real estate columnist, said, "On a scale of 1 to 10 this book rates a 10."

Our fifth book, *Going Going Gone! Auctioning Your Home for Top Dollar* (2001), was also written to benefit the homeowner in the selling of a home. Like *How to Sell Your Home Without a Broker,* our auctioning book was designed to show you how to successfully sell your home and net the most money.

Our sixth book, *The New Path to Real Estate Wealth: Earning Without Owning* (2004), was our first book designed specifically for active real estate investors. Our real estate investing titles are designed to take you from being a novice real estate investor to being an expert real estate investor.

The New Path to Real Estate Wealth: Earning Without Owning takes you from the real estate basics through the four best ways to make money in real estate. From flipping property to assigning contracts to controlling property using options to buying discount mortgage paper, it teaches you everything you need to know to become a successful real estate investor. In all four areas, we train you how to make money without buying or owning property!

Our premise for our real estate investing books is that no matter what kind of real estate investment you are going to make, you have to win going in. It is no longer enough to make money on the back end of a deal or make a profit when you get out of a deal. The deal has to have a profit built in on the front end, or else you shouldn't do it at all.

Our seventh book, *Quick Cash in Foreclosures* (2004), was picked by Robert J. Bruss as one of his top-10 real estate books of 2004. In it we show you how to make money going into a foreclosure deal. It is a hands-on book that teaches you how to enter the real estate foreclosure market and make deals happen. What is unique about the book is that we show you how to have a quick-cash investment strategy that you can successfully implement with little or no investment capital.

Our philosophy is that if you want to be active in your investment life, you must be in control of your investments. Counting on a stockbroker, investment adviser, accountant, general partner, or real estate investment fund leaves you completely out of control. When you are an active real estate investor, you are the one calling the shots. You are the one responsible for your successes and failures.

Our eighth book, *Make Money in Real Estate Tax Liens: How to Guarantee Returns Up to 50%* (2005), teaches you how to make money investing in real estate tax liens. Once a real estate tax lien is placed against real property, one of two things will happen.

Either the lien will be paid off by the owner of the property or an investor will buy the lien from the taxing agency that filed it. If the owner of the property does not redeem the lien from the investor, the investor can foreclose on the property and gain an ownership interest.

By investing in real estate tax liens, for pennies on the dollar, you can control a property. Your guarantee is you have the power of foreclosure in the event you are not paid back your original tax lien investment plus hefty interest and penalties. Investing in real estate tax liens is definitely a win going in!

Our ninth book, *Make Money in Short-Sale Foreclosures: How to Bypass Owners and Buy Directly from Lenders* (2006) focuses on how to make money investing in short-sale foreclosures.

A short-sale foreclosure is a mortgage lender accepting less for the loan balance due as a payoff for the loan. Typically, loans are made for no more than 80 percent of the value of the property. In a short-sale, you are buying the property for less than the loan amount. This is buying real estate at a wholesale price.

By investing in short-sale foreclosures, you can bypass the owners and buy directly from the lenders. You can do this before, during, or after the foreclosure sale. Whichever way you choose to become involved and invest in short-sale foreclosures, you can make money.

Make Money in Abandoned Properties shows readers how to make money investing in abandoned properties.

Owners abandon properties for three main reasons. These include financial reasons, death or divorce, and when the property becomes uninhabitable. Whatever the reasons, there is an opportunity for you to make money.

This book will show you how to systematically find abandoned properties, locate the owners who have abandoned the properties, and write a foolproof offer. You will learn how to present your offer and negotiate with the owners to have your offer accepted. We will show you how to obtain financing to hold or rehab the property. Finally, we will discuss how to find motivated buyers for your property.

We recommend you read this book in a particular way. Bring a lot of energy to your reading. This doesn't mean that you have to necessarily read the book quickly, though that is fine with us. We want you to be excited about the material. We want you to win going in as you read.

We suggest that if you find yourself bogging down, stop reading. The material is designed to be comprehended in bursts. See if you can go from one lightbulb turning on in your mind to the next. As it gets brighter and brighter, you will find yourself energized.

Our purpose for writing our real estate investing books is to share with you all our real estate knowledge and expertise. We want to be the Brain Trust for your successful real estate investments and your lucrative financial investments. The concepts in this book, like all our books, are applicable to most types of real estate just about anywhere.

Whether you invest in foreclosures, mortgage notes, apartment buildings, or abandoned properties, our goal is for you to get started. You will know you are a successful investor after you make money on your first real estate deal.

We would love to hear from you about your successes. Also, we want to hear what is working and what is not working for you. Please e-mail us at thetrustee@hotmail.com or contact us through our publisher, John Wiley & Sons. We are available to help you put your deals together. We are available to partner deals. We also offer various educational and investment programs. Good luck and good deals!

Chantal & Bill Carey

CHAPTER 1

What Is Abandoned Property?

Have you ever been driving through your neighborhood and noticed a property that looked like it needed some work? Perhaps the fence had some pickets missing. The garage door could use a new coat of paint. Maybe the grass was three weeks past being mowed. Newspapers were accumulating in the driveway. Multiple pizza flyers were rubber-banded to the handle of the front door.

Is this a property wherein the owners have no pride of ownership? Is the property owner's lawn mower in the repair shop? Is this a property of owners who went on a vacation and forgot to stop the newspaper? Do these property owners never go in and out the front door? Or is this a property that has been abandoned by the owners?

Your curiosity gets the better of you. You decide to watch the property to see if anyone is coming or going. You see no signs of human activity. You drive by at night to see if there are any lights on. The property is always dark.

One day you decide to stop and ring the doorbell. No one answers. You notice the bird droppings on the front stoop from the nest in the entry eaves. Talk about disgusting. Why don't the property owners clean up this mess? They are not around to notice. The property owners have walked away from their property.

Abandoned Property

Every neighborhood in every city or town has abandoned property. These properties can be single-family residential, condominiums, duplexes, triplexes, fourplexes, apartments, commercial, industrial, business, hotels, resorts, farms, ranches, or vacant land. Any category of real estate you can think of contains abandoned property.

Abandoned property can be found in big cities. Abandoned property can be found in rural areas. Abandoned property can be found in small towns. Abandoned property can be found along the coast. Abandoned property can be found in the mountains. You can find abandoned property anywhere.

Physical Condition

An abandoned property can be in distressed condition. Abandoned property can fit into a stereotype of a property that looks blighted or run-down. An abandoned property can be in a bad neighborhood. Abandoned property can be on the wrong side of the tracks.

An abandoned property can be in good condition. Abandoned property can be outside the stereotype and be in immaculate condition. An abandoned property can be in a good neighborhood. Abandoned property can be on the right side of the tracks.

Title Condition

An abandoned property can be about to go into foreclosure. Abandoned property can be in foreclosure. An abandoned property can have unpaid property taxes. Abandoned property can have federal tax liens, state tax liens, and judgment liens against the title.

An abandoned property can have loans that are in good standing. Abandoned property can have property taxes that are paid current. An abandoned property can have no tax liens or judgment liens against the title. In fact, abandoned property can have completely clear title.

Ownership

The property owners of abandoned property are individuals, families, general partnerships, limited partnerships, family partnerships, corporations, trusts, small businesses, big businesses, local, state, and national governments. The abandoned-property owners can be local to the community, live in the next town, live out of state or out of the country.

Abandoned-property owners can be banks, mutual funds, stock cooperatives, local property-taxing authorities, foreign investors, the Internal Revenue Service, nonprofit organizations, churches, synagogues, mosques.

Any entity you can think of can be an abandoned-property owner. An abandoned-property owner can be a celebrity or a nobody. An abandoned-property owner can be a royal or a commoner. An abandoned-property owner can be a legal business entity or an illegal business entity.

Financial

Abandoned-property owners are poor. Abandoned-property owners are rich. Abandoned-property owners are everything in between rich and poor. The owners of abandoned property can fit into a stereotype of being financially strapped or even destitute.

The abandoned-property owner can be in bankruptcy or about to be in bankruptcy. An abandoned-property owner can also be completely outside the stereotype and be quite well off financially.

Beyond the Stereotype

Our point is that we want you to expand beyond your stereotypical sensibilities when it comes to finding and buying abandoned property. Yes, we agree that your initial notion of what an abandoned property would look like and who an abandoned-property owner would be is a good starting point for your investing in abandoned property.

That is why we started this chapter out the way we did. However, an abandoned property can feel and seem like a normal property and look like other normal properties in the area. An abandoned property can even have someone living in it! How does that expand you beyond your stereotypical sensibilities?

Sixth Sense

We also want you to develop an abandoned-property sixth sense. This will allow you to find and buy abandoned property that other real estate investors never identified as abandoned property. Because the abandoned property was outside of their stereotypical sensibilities, your potential competition becomes no competition for you!

This sixth sense is like the sixth sense we want you to develop in our book *Make Money in Short-Sale Foreclosures* (John Wiley & Sons, 2006). In that book, we show you how to identify short-sale foreclosure opportunities with property that does not fit the stereotypical real estate foreclosure investor's sensibilities. You will develop this sixth sense in the abandoned-property arena by reading this book.

Undiscovered Gold Mine

The first prospectors in California in the 1840s were ahead of their time. Very few people had the dream or the vision to pan for gold in the streams and creeks of the foothills of the Sierra Nevadas on the east side of San Francisco Bay. The work could be lonely, difficult, and the object of ridicule by people in the know who knew that the prospectors were wasting their time.

In 1849, gold was discovered at Sutter's Mill. This was the beginning of the California gold rush. It turned out that there was gold in them thar' hills! Today, the professional football team in San Francisco is called the San Francisco 49ers in recognition of those prospectors, known as forty-niners, who put San Francisco on the map. Needless to say, the prospectors who staked out their claims early were the ones who were more likely to strike it rich.

Abandoned property is the undiscovered real estate investment gold mine of the next three to five years. Just as the gold in California was already there waiting to be discovered, abandoned property is already there in your area waiting to be discovered. And who better to discover it than you?

Real Estate People in the Know

Real estate people in the know have yet to put their seal of approval on abandoned property as a legitimate real estate investment opportunity. They are waiting for the news media to announce there is an abandoned-property market. That is the good news for you and us. For those of us who can see the abandoned-property opportunity, we will be able to stake our claim now.

We will be more likely to strike it rich than those who jump on the abandoned-property bandwagon in the years to come. This will be long after we have discovered gold in them thar' abandoned-property hills.

Amount of Abandoned Property

To quantify the amount of abandoned property is a difficult task. As is usually the case, statistics are created after a reality has already occurred. Abandoned-property statistics are no different. As we were researching this book, we found we were finding abandoned property that was abandoned in the real world but had not yet been counted as abandoned property in the world of statistics. For those of you who want numbers, we estimate that somewhere between 1 percent and 2 percent of property is or will become abandoned over the next three years. As you know, all real estate markets are ultimately local in nature. The abandoned property in your real estate market will be local to that market. The statistics could be higher. To give you access to the amount of abandoned property in your area, we are going to tell you a story that we think all of you can relate to.

New Car Experience

How many of you have had the following experience? You decide it is time to buy a new car. You go to the dealer showroom and find just the car for you. It is the perfect color, has all the features you want, the dealer offers you what you need for your trade-in, and you get the price and financing terms to fit your budget.

You make the deal and drive off the lot in your new car. You are feeling excited, breathing in that new-car smell, and can't wait to show off your new baby to your family and friends. Not to mention the drool factor from other drivers in the lane beside you at the stoplights.

Driving home, you see your model car within a mile or two of the dealership. Before you get home, you may see one or two other cars that are your model car, even one that is the exact same color! What is odd is that before you bought your new car you had never seen any other models like it.

Abandoned-property investing is similar to the new-car experience that we have just described. Before you decide to investigate investing in the abandoned-property arena, you may have driven by at least three or four abandoned properties and not even seen them. You had no idea that these properties were abandoned.

Once you decide to make your first abandoned-property investment, you start seeing abandoned properties everywhere you go. Your abandoned-property sixth sense kicks in. We can be driving through a neighborhood or area and know within 30 seconds if a property is abandoned. With practice, in a very short period of time you will be able to do the same.

Prediction

We predict that the abandoned-property market is going to explode. Every market is predicated on supply and demand. The abandoned-property market is no different. On the supply side, both from a reality standpoint and a statistical standpoint, the supply of abandoned property is going to increase. We will address where this increase will come from in Chapter 2, "Why Do Property Owners Walk Away?"

For our discussion purposes here, what we want you to get is that when the supply of abandoned property increases, the price or cost of the abandoned property will decrease. This is good news for us as abandoned-property investors. As abandoned-property investors, we want to buy as low as we can and sell as high as we can.

Amount of Money You Can Make in Abandoned Property

The amount of money you can make investing in abandoned property is unlimited. We are going to give you three examples from abandoned-property deals we have been involved with. This will give you a sense of the range of the amount of money you can make investing in abandoned property.

We have made as little as $5,000 investing in abandoned property. We have made as much as $100,000 investing in abandoned property. One of the best deals we made in abandoned property was a deal we didn't make. That deal would have cost us $1 million.

$5,000 Abandoned-Property Deal

We made $5,000 on an abandoned one-bedroom condo in Del Mar, California. The property owner was a real estate investor who lived in Arizona. The investor had bought the condo two years before and had it rented on a lease option. After 18 months, the tenant was transferred out of town and did not exercise their option to purchase.

We came on the scene after the condo had been vacant for six months. We contacted the owner in Arizona. The owner had pretty much forgotten about this condo. His real estate investing had shifted into bigger commercial projects.

About the only connection he had with the condo was writing the yearly check for the homeowner's association dues and paying the property taxes twice a year. The investor owned the condo free and clear. There were no monthly mortgage payments. This condo was an abandoned property.

We valued the condo at $95,000. We wrote an all-cash offer for $80,000. We write all our real estate contracts with an assignment clause. (We will go over this in detail for you in Chapter 14, "Assigning Your Abandoned-Property Deals.")

This would give us the ability to assign our interest in the contract to a third party for an assignment fee if the property owner accepted our offer. When the abandoned-property owner accepted our offer, we had an instant $15,000 equity position in the property.

Instant Equity Position

Condo Value	$95,000
Our Offer	−$80,000
Instant Equity Position	$15,000

Did we want to pay $80,000 cash for this condo? No, we did not. We found another investor to whom we assigned our interest in the accepted contract for a $5,000 assignment fee.

Assignment of Accepted Contract

Our Assignment Fee $5,000

The investor to whom we assigned our contract proceeded to close the transaction with the abandoned-property owner for $80,000. Their total investment in the property was now $85,000.

Investor Total Investment

Our Assignment Fee	$5,000
Contract Price	+$80,000
Investor Total Investment	$85,000

This was a win/win/win deal. The abandoned-property owner disposed of his abandoned property. We made $5,000 for finding and buying (assigning our contract) an abandoned property. The investor to whom we assigned our abandoned property contract had a $10,000 equity position.

Investor Equity Position

Condo Value	$95,000
Investor Total Investment	−$85,000
Investor Equity Position	$10,000

$100,000 Abandoned-Property Deal

We made $100,000 on abandoned vacant land in the great state of Texas. We say the *great state of Texas* for two reasons. The first reason is that outside of Alaska, Texas is the definition of great, as in vast. There is lots of vacant land in Texas.

The second reason we say the *great state of Texas* is because we live in Texas and like doing abandoned-property deals here. As in *great* abandoned-property deals.

One day when we were driving, we found a for-sale-by-owner sign that looked a little the worse for wear. The sign was on what appeared to be vacant land. We could barely make out the phone number on the sign. When we called the number, it had been disconnected.

We checked the property-tax records and got a name and an address for the property owner. We tried getting a phone number, but again no luck. So we wrote a letter to the property owner saying we were interested in buying their property.

Three months went by, and frankly we had forgotten about the sign, the property, and our letter. We then received a letter from the property owner. They were interested in selling us the property. It was a 100-acre parcel. The price they wanted was $4,500 per acre. This would be a total of $450,000.

Vacant Land Deal

Price per Acre	$4,500
Number of Acres	× 100
Total Price	$450,000

The reason it had taken so long for the property owner to get back to us was they were the out-of-state relatives of the Texas owner. The Texas owner had passed away, and the out-of-state relatives had inherited the property. None of them was interested in coming to Texas to take over the property. Essentially, they wanted the cash out of the property to split between six heirs.

The original sign we saw on the property had the phone number of the Texas owner who had passed away. He had been trying to sell the property to pay for medical expenses. This was a sad story but real life in the abandoned-property investing arena.

We did a market analysis of the acreage and determined it was worth $5,500 an acre. We wrote an option contract on the property with a six-month option period that would pay $450,000 in cash to the out-of-state heirs if we exercised our option. (We will get into options in Chapter 16.)

We found a buyer in four months who agreed to purchase the property from us for $550,000. We exercised our option with the heirs for $450,000 and made $100,000 on the deal.

Sold Property For	$550,000
Bought Property For	−$450,000
Our Profit	$100,000

The $1 Million Abandoned-Property Deal

Sometimes the best abandoned-property deal you make is the abandoned-property deal you don't make. We saved $1 million by not buying an abandoned hotel in Biloxi, Mississippi.

In 2003, while traveling through the Mississippi Gulf Coast, we found an abandoned hotel in Biloxi, Mississippi. It was on the Gulf of Mexico across the street from the water. Casinos were located within a stone's throw of the hotel's entrance.

We were staying in a small hotel that was adjacent to the abandoned hotel. We noticed a for sale sign on what looked like a vacant lot on the other side of the hotel where we were staying. We asked the hotel manager if he knew anything about the property for sale. We discovered that what was for sale was the vacant lot, the small hotel, and what turned out to be a six-story abandoned hotel next door.

The hotel manager had the keys and offered to show us the big hotel. We were immediately enamored with this 1920s diamond in the rough. We found out the owner lived 100 miles away. We made contact and set up an appointment to meet. The abandoned-property owner owned the property free and clear. He had owned the hotel for nine years. Unfortunately, he had suffered a heart attack in 2002.

The plans this property owner had to restore the hotel had been abandoned after he suffered his heart attack. As is, the hotel and the land were worth $4.75 million. We could buy the property for $3.5 million. If we would make a $1 million cash down payment, the owner would seller-finance a carry-back first mortgage for $2.5 million.

Hotel Deal

Purchase Price	$3,500,000
Down Payment	−$1,000,000
Seller First Mortgage	$2,500,000

We would have a $1.25 million equity position going into the deal.

Our Equity Position

Hotel Value	$4,750,000
Purchase Price	−$3,500,000
Our Equity Position	$1,250,000

We were actually getting very excited about doing this deal. We wanted to take on the project of restoring the hotel. The owner was excited because he could see that by selling us the hotel we could help him regain his abandoned dream of restoring the hotel to its former elegance.

We wound up not doing this deal. There was no good real estate reason not to do this deal. Even if we decided not to go through with the restoration, we still would have been able to make money just flipping or holding onto the property.

Our sixth sense kicked in, and we just had a gut feeling not to proceed. The owner was disappointed. He actually became angry with us when we could not articulate any reasonable explanation for not going through with the deal.

The down payment was doable. The seller financing was fantastic. We would have an instant equity position. There was everything to like from an abandoned-property real estate investment perspective.

Two and a half years later, we found out why we couldn't do the hotel deal in Biloxi, Mississippi. Hurricane Katrina roared through and destroyed the hotel. All the work of restoration would have been ruined. We could have lost many millions of dollars.

Even with insurance, because of the deductible we would have been out at least $1 million. We had saved ourselves two-and-a-half years, heartache, and financial discomfort. This has been our best abandoned-property deal so far. Thank you, sixth sense!

In the next chapter, we will talk about why property owners walk away from or abandon their property. We have found that property owners walk away from their property for three main reasons. These three reasons include financial reasons, death or divorce, and an uninhabitable property.

CHAPTER 2

Why Do Property Owners Walk Away?

Why do property owners walk away from their property? At first glance, the answer seems to lie in the domain of insanity. You would have to be crazy to walk away from a property you own. Let's take the simplest case of a person buying a home and look at the work involved just to get into the property.

The amount of time and work it takes to locate a property you like and can afford is emotionally and financially burdensome. Then you have to go through the negotiation process with the seller. This can entail offers and counteroffers and counteroffers to the counteroffers.

After you have your offer or counteroffer accepted, then you have to qualify for and obtain a real estate loan. Then come the loan applications, credit checks, appraisals, and going through loan committees.

Simultaneously, you open an escrow that entails signing escrow instructions, having termite inspections, contractor inspections, walk-through inspections, signing amended escrow instructions and loan documents, then coming up with down payments and closing costs, and finally closing.

Once you close escrow and receive the keys to the property, then the real fun begins. You have to pack all your stuff and move! You have to transfer the utilities, forward the mail, change schools if you have kids, stop and start the newspaper. It goes on and on.

You are in the property for two years. You have paid two years of loan payments, property taxes, and homeowner's insurance. Then one day you wake up and say, "Today is the day I am walking away from my property." Yes, you must be totally insane. Or you have one or more good reasons that will make you walk away from the property that you have worked so hard to acquire and hold.

Property Owners Walk Away for Three Main Reasons

Property owners abandon their property for three main reasons. The first reason property owners abandon their property is because of financial problems. The second reason that property owners abandon their property is because of death or divorce. The third reason property owners abandon their property is because the property becomes uninhabitable.

1. Financial Problems

The number-one reason property owners walk away from their property is due to financial problems. Typically, a job loss leads to a downward financial spiral. A job transfer can also cause financial hardship. There may be an injury or illness in the family that creates a huge money problem. Rather than face the embarrassment of a foreclosure and forcible eviction, the owners abandon their property and move on.

Normally, this situation is found in single-family residential situations. However, financial problems can affect corporate and government owners that own large properties, too. Individual job losses may be due to a plant or military base closure. (General Motors and fill in your military base.)

Corporate malfeasance may lead to huge financial problems for a company (Enron, WorldCom, Adelphia, and so on). Technological change may make a company and its product obsolete overnight (think telecommunications industry).

2. Death or Divorce

The second reason owners abandon their property is death or divorce. Besides the financial burden, it may become too unbearable psychologically or emotionally for the surviving or remaining owner to stay in the property.

A property owner could die in the property. Someone could be killed on a property. Someone from the past could have died or been killed on a property. Once the current owners discover these facts, this can make them feel unable to continue to live or work on the property. We have encountered owners who have abandoned their property because they felt the property was haunted!

3. Property Becomes Uninhabitable

The third reason owners abandon their property is because the property becomes uninhabitable. There may be a major environmental problem that affects an entire neighborhood. Or one of the owners or family members may develop an allergic reaction to the property itself. Over the next five years, people becoming allergic to their homes or work environments is going to develop into a major health problem recognized by the general public.

Finally, a weather-related catastrophe or a fire can also make a property uninhabitable. Property owners in Texas and the Gulf Coast states are still reeling from the impact of Hurricanes Rita and Katrina. If the owners are uninsured or underinsured, they may elect to abandon the property rather than rebuild.

Opportunity to Make Money

Whatever the reasons for the owners to abandon their property, there is an opportunity for the savvy investor to make money. We will show you how to find abandoned properties and locate the owners by being observant and doing some investigating. We will then teach you how to negotiate with the owners to get the title to the property.

It has been our experience that when you present the owners a solution to their unresolved property problem, the owners will take it. We tell the owners that even though they have abandoned their property, ultimately, if they have a loan on the property, their lender will foreclose. By making a deal with us, the foreclosure will be avoided.

We tell owners who have no loans on their property that the local taxing authority will foreclose on their property for back property taxes even though the owners have abandoned the property. By making a deal with us, the property-tax fore-closure will be avoided.

To make money investing in abandoned property, you must make your offer based on your analysis of value. You are an investor buying at a wholesale price. As an investor, you cannot pay a retail price. Make your low offer and let the abandoned-property owner decide whether they will take your offer.

How does an investor know that they are buying low? An investor knows they are buying low because a real estate investor knows value. Your mission as a real estate investor is to become an expert in valuing all the different types of real estate in your target area.

Target Area

We recommend that you have a target area that you concentrate on for your abandoned-property investing. This target area is a geographic area. Most real estate investors concentrate on a particular type of real estate. This ranges from residential property to industrial property to commercial property to vacant land.

The visual image we would like you to get is that of dropping a stone in a pond. A wave pattern of concentric circles begins to radiate outward from where the stone hits the water. Your target area consists of these ever-widening concentric circles.

At first we recommend you concentrate on a target area that may be 5 or 10 miles across. Then continue to expand your target area outward. Your goal is to catch any and all of the abandoned property in the net of your target area.

What we are saying is that once you identify a target area for your abandoned-property investing, any type of abandoned property becomes fair game. Abandoned houses, condos, land, apartment buildings, hotels. In other words, the particular type of real estate you are looking for in your target area is abandoned property, any kind of abandoned property. Our target area is the Dallas–Fort Worth metroplex. This covers a circle 35 miles across.

Knowing Value

Are you ready to become an expert in valuing real estate? We are going to take you step by step through the knowledge we have gained in our combined fifty-plus years as real estate investors valuing real estate.

We will define the six values that every real estate investor needs to know about property they are investing in. We will show you the three ways to value real estate that are used by real estate appraisers. We will explain the four elements of real estate value that are unique to the real estate market.

Next, we will reveal the four great forces that influence real estate value. Finally, we will teach you the seven ways to know value in your target area. You must know value to be successful investing in abandoned property.

The Six Values Every Real Estate Investor Needs to Know

There are six values every real estate investor needs to know about property they are investing in. These are so important that we reiterate them in each of our books. We can't stress valuation enough. These six values are the retail value, the wholesale value, the replacement value, the property-tax value, the loan value, and the appraised value.

1. Retail Value

The retail value is the value an end user, like a homeowner, places on a piece of real estate. The retail value tends to be the highest value of all the values placed on real estate.

2. Wholesale Value

The wholesale value is the value a real estate investor, like you, places on a piece of real estate. The wholesale value tends to be the lowest value of all the values placed on real estate.

3. Replacement Value

The replacement value is the value insurance companies place on the improvements on a piece of real estate. The replacement value is determined by the cost approach.

4. Property-Tax Value

The property-tax value is the value the local property-tax assessor places on a piece of real estate. The property-tax value could be higher or lower than the retail value.

5. Loan Value

The loan value is the value a real estate lender, like a bank or mortgage company, places on a piece of real estate. The loan value tends to vary as a percentage of the appraised value.

6. Appraised Value

The appraised value is the value a real estate appraiser places on a piece of property. The appraised value is typically at or near the retail value.

Three Ways to Value Real Estate

There are three ways to value real estate. The three ways are the cost approach, the income approach, and the market-comparison approach. When a real estate appraiser makes an appraisal, the appraiser will use one, two, or possibly all three of these valuation approaches.

1. Cost Approach

The cost approach consists of three parts. First, value the land. Second, value the improvements on the land, such as buildings, and add the value of the improvements to the value of the land. Third, determine the accrued depreciation of the improvements and subtract the accrued depreciation from the combined value of the land and improvements.

Cost Approach Example

Let's look at an example. If the land is valued at $200,000, the improvements are valued at $450,000, and the accrued depreciation is $125,000, what is the value of the property according to the cost approach?

Land Value	$200,000
Improvements	+$450,000
Total	$650,000
Accrued Depreciation	−$125,000
Property Value	$525,000

We added the value of the improvements, $450,000, to the value of the land, $200,000, and got $650,000. We then subtracted the accrued depreciation, $125,000, and came up with a property value of $525,000.

2. Income Approach

The income approach uses the income a property produces to determine its value. We say it this way: The value of an income property is in direct relationship to the income the property produces.

Gross Rent Multiplier

Let's look at an example. The gross rent multiplier says the value of an income-producing property is determined by the gross annual rent the property receives multiplied by the gross rent multiplier.

You can find out the gross rent multiplier for your area by calling a commercial real estate company and asking them what the gross rent multiplier is for your city. If the gross annual rent is $240,000 and the gross rent multiplier for the area is 9, then we multiply $240,000 by 9 and come up with a value of $2,160,000.

Gross Rent	$240,000
Gross Rent Multiplier	× 9
Value	$2,160,000

Another way to determine value using the income approach is with the formula value = income/capitalization rate. In this case, the income is the net operating income (NOI for short), which is the gross income minus the operating expenses. The capitalization rate is determined by the market in the area the property is located.

Let's say the gross income the property generated on an annual basis is $240,000. If the operating expenses for the property for the year are $75,000, then the net operating income for the property is $165,000.

Gross Income	$240,000
Operating Expenses	−$75,000
Net Operating Income	$165,000

Capitalization Rate

For example, in Dallas, Texas, real estate investors might require an 8.5 percent capitalization rate, and in Phoenix, Arizona, real estate investors might require a 9.5 percent capitalization rate.

You can find out the capitalization rate for your area by calling a commercial real estate company and asking them what the capitalization rate is in your city.

If the net operating income is $165,000 and the capitalization rate is 8.5 percent (Dallas, Texas), then the value of the property is $1,941,000 ($165,000/.085 = $1,941,000). If the property is located in Phoenix, Arizona, however, with the same $1,941,000 net operating income, then the value of the property is only $1,737,000 ($165,000/.095 = $1,737,000).

Dallas, Texas		**Phoenix, Arizona**
	Net Operating	
$165,000	Income	$165,000
.085	Capitalization Rate	.095
$1,941,000	Property Value	$1,737,000

3. Market-Comparison Approach

The market-comparison approach uses the value of similar properties to determine the value of a particular property. How many of you have heard the expression *comps*? Comps is short for *comparable properties.* You compare properties that are similar to the property you are interested in to determine its value. We say it this way: "No comps, no contract."

Market-Comparison Example

Let's look at an example. If you are trying to determine the value of a three-bedroom, two-bathroom, 1,600 square foot, attached two-car garage home, you compare it to as similar properties as you can find that have sold within the last 180 days in the neighborhood.

Property 1 is a three-bedroom, two-bathroom, 1,625 square foot, attached two-car garage home that sold for $245,000 45 days ago. Property 2 is a three-bedroom, two-bathroom, 1,575 square foot, attached two-car garage home that sold for $290,000 60 days ago. Property 3 is a three-bedroom, two-bathroom, 1,700 square foot, attached two-car garage home that sold for $305,000 30 days ago.

The price per square foot for each of these properties is $171.44 ($245,000/1,625 square feet is $150.77; $290,000/ 1,575 square feet is $184.13; $305,000/1,700 square feet is $179.41). If we multiply our 1,600 square feet by $171.44, we get a value of $274,304 for the property we are looking at.

Property 1	**Property 2**	**Property 3**
$245,000	$290,000	$305,000
1,625	1,575	1,700
$150.77	$184.13	$179.41

Subject Property

1,600 Square Feet
× $171.44
$274,304

This, of course, is a summary chart of the market-comparison example information. To help you determine the most accurate values of properties you are analyzing, you may want to use a form to organize the information you gather.

Four Elements of Value

There are four elements of value in real estate. They are demand, utility, scarcity, and transferability. These four elements of value constitute the value of a piece of real estate. We use the acronym *DUST* as a memory aid to keep the four elements of value in mind.

1. Demand

Demand is the first element of value. Demand is the number of people who want the property. The more people who want the property, the more valuable the property becomes.

2. Utility

Utility is the second element of value. Utility is the use that a property can be put to or made of. The more uses that a property can be put to or made of, the more valuable the property.

3. Scarcity

Scarcity is the third element of value. Scarcity has to do with the supply of real estate available. This supply could be what is on the market or the total possible number of properties in an area. The scarcer the supply of real estate available, the more valuable the property.

4. Transferability

Transferability is the fourth element of value. Transferability is the key element of value in real estate. You can have the best property in the world, worth millions of dollars, but if you cannot transfer the title to your property to a buyer, then you have no sale. Likewise if you are a real estate buyer and have written a great wholesale offer that has been accepted by the seller, your deal is worthless unless you can get the seller to transfer clear property title to you.

Four Great Forces that Influence Value

There are four great forces that influence the value of real estate. They are physical forces, economic forces, political forces, and social forces. These four great forces are present in every real estate market in the country. These four forces can have a great impact on the amount and kind of abandoned property in your target area.

1. Physical Forces

Physical forces are the first of the great forces that influence the value of real estate. The availability of schools, shopping, churches, transportation, and parks are physical forces that influence real estate value. If these physical amenities are present in your target area, this influences the value of the area in an upward manner. If these physical amenities are not present or are minimally present in your target area, this influences the value of the area in a downward manner.

2. Economic Forces

Economic forces are the second of the great forces that influence the value of real estate. The number and types of jobs available, the wages paid, where in the economic cycle the economy is nationally, and the interest rates for real estate loans are economic forces that influence real estate value.

The economic cycle is a repeating expansion, prosperity, recession, depression cycle. Real estate value is greatly influenced by the economic cycle. Typically, real estate is said to do well in the expansion and prosperity phases of the economic cycle, and real estate is said to do poorly in the recession and depression phases of the economic cycle.

3. Political Forces

Political forces are the third of the great forces that influence the value of real estate. The types of zoning, pro-growth or no-growth policies, and environmental regulations are political forces that influence the value of real estate.

It is important for you to know the political forces that influence the value of real estate in your area. This is for the present investment climate and for the future investment climate.

4. Social Forces

Social forces are the fourth of the great forces that influence the value of real estate. The quality of the schools and the number in the area, blighted neighborhoods or well-kept neighborhoods, racial or ethnic strife, and social amenities are the social forces that influence the value of real estate.

Seven Ways to Know Value in Your Target Area

There are seven ways to know value in your target area. They are sold comparables, pending comparables, listed comparables, expired comparables, appreciation rates, new or planned development, and vacancy rates.

1. Sold Comparables

Sold comparables are the first way to know value in your target area. Sold comparables set the floor of retail value for real estate. This means that if a sold comparable sold for $125,000, a similar property should sell for no lower than $125,000 in a normal real estate market.

Sold comparables as the name implies are properties that have been sold and have actually closed escrow. Sold comparables are useful for properties that have sold in the last six months. Anything beyond six months is not considered a good comparable.

2. Pending Comparables

Pending comparables are the second way to know value in your target area. Pending comparables indicate the direction of real estate value. A pending comparable is a property that has sold but has not closed escrow. When the pending comparable closes escrow, it will become a sold comparable. If the sold comparables are indicating a value of $125,000 and the pending comparables are indicating a value of $127,000 then you are getting an indication that the direction of real estate values is going up.

3. Listed Comparables

Listed comparables are the third way to know value in your target area. Listed comparables set the ceiling of retail value for real estate. Listed comparables are properties that are currently on the market and are similar to property in which you are considering investing.

Listed comparables set the ceiling of value because they have neither sold nor closed escrow. They are merely an indicator of what sellers would like to get for their properties.

4. Expired Comparables

Expired comparables are the fourth way to know value in your target area. Expired comparables are property listings that indicate the value that is beyond the present market in terms of what retail real estate buyers are willing to pay for property.

Retail buyers will buy the lower-priced comparable properties first, all things being equal. Expired comparables are properties that never sold, let alone closed escrow.

5. Appreciation Rates

Appreciation rates are the fifth way to know value in your target area. Appreciation rates give you a sense of how hot or cold the real estate market is. Double-digit appreciation rates indicate a hot real estate market. Single-digit appreciation rates indicate a good real estate market. Zero or negative appreciation rates indicate a cold real estate market.

6. *New or Planned Developments*

New or planned developments are the sixth way to know value in your target area. By studying the path of new development and buying property in the path of that development, you can ensure that you are buying property that is going to appreciate in value.

7. *Vacancy Rates*

Vacancy rates are the seventh way to know value in your target area. High vacancy rates indicate an area that may have problem properties. Low vacancy rates indicate an area that may have profitable properties.

Let's summarize what we learned in this chapter. In spite of how difficult it is to get into a property, owners walk away from their property. Property owners walk away from their property for three main reasons. These include financial reasons, death or divorce, and when a property becomes uninhabitable.

We recommended that you have a target area for your abandoned property investing. This target area is a circle within which you will look for any type of property that is abandoned. If you are more comfortable working residential property or commercial property or vacant land, however, then please work in your comfort zone.

We concluded with an in-depth look at knowing value. We repeat what we said earlier: You must know value to be successful investing in abandoned property. Just because a property has been abandoned doesn't mean it is a good deal. You make it a good deal by knowing value.

In the next chapter, we will talk about motivated property owners. A motivated property owner is the key to making money in abandoned property. We define a motivated property owner as a property owner in distress. A property owner in distress may be one step away from being an abandoned-property owner.

CHAPTER 3

Motivated Abandoned-Property Owners

A motivated abandoned-property owner is the key to making money in abandoned property. In this chapter we will teach you how to find motivated property owners. You have to be a pretty good detective if you are going to be a successful real estate investor. You have to be a great detective if you are going to be successful investing in abandoned property.

We define a motivated property owner as a property owner in distress. A property owner in distress may be one step away from being an abandoned-property owner. Obviously, abandoned-property owners own abandoned property. Find a property owner in distress and you are on your way to finding an abandoned property.

We are going to give you the 13 key words or phrases that we look for when we go through classified ads, work with our personal contacts, do our own scouting, visit open houses, or work with a real estate agent. When you see or hear one or more of these words or phrases, you'll know that you have likely found a property owner in distress. We will then conclude this chapter with a discussion about motivated property owners in foreclosure.

Finding Property Owners in Distress

We have already mentioned that the clues to property owners in distress include deferred maintenance on a property or the look of a property being abandoned. Other clues are general lack of care by the owner or tenant and frequent official deliveries of notices to pay or posted utility shutoffs or foreclosure notices.

It takes a keen eye to observe some of these subtle hints to an impending abandoned-property condition. Neighbors and service providers such as delivery companies, utility providers, and postal carriers can be your extra eyes and ears. Postal carriers know everything that goes on in a neighborhood.

13 Key Words or Phrases

1. Must Sell

Any time you encounter the phrase *must sell,* you have come upon the property owner in distress. It is perfectly acceptable to ask the must-sell property owner why they must sell. We have found that if you ask, people will usually be quite forthcoming about why they must sell.

2. Under Market

The phrase *under market* can let you know that you have come on the right property owner and the right property. As a real estate investor you are a wholesale buyer. A property that is advertised as being under market puts you ahead of the game from the get-go.

3. Below Appraisal

Below appraisal is a phrase we like to hear. This occurs when a real estate agent tells us the property they are marketing for the property owner is priced below the appraisal value. We know we may have the right property and the right property owner.

4. Transferred

Transferred can mean "transferred." Or transferred can be a code word for a property owner in distress. In today's economy, when someone is transferred, they are often happy to have a job to be transferred to.

5. Divorce

When you see or hear the word *divorce,* there is often a real estate deal close by. There are two to three million new marriages each year in the United States. There are one to one-and-a-half million divorces. What happens to the family home when a divorce occurs? Statistics tell us that in a divorce most real estate winds up being sold so that the assets can be divided between the former spouses.

6. Foreclosure Ad

Usually, you see something like this in a real estate classified ad:

> Seller in foreclosure.
> Bring all offers.
> 4Br/3Ba $475,000.
> Good area.
> (817) 555-2455.

Call about the ad. Identify yourself as a real estate investor. Find out when the foreclosure sale is scheduled. Set an appointment to meet with the property owner to show them their foreclosure options. If they have equity in the property, make an offer to buy their equity. If they have little or no equity in the property make a short-sale offer. (For a complete discussion of short-sale foreclosures, see our book *Make Money in Short-Sale Foreclosures* [John Wiley & Sons, 2006].)

7. *Illness Ad*

Unfortunately, illness is a fact of life. Sometimes your job as a real estate investor can really help people out of a tough situation. A real estate ad we saw read something like this:

> Illness forces sale.
> Great family home in good area.
> Priced to sell. $525,000.
> Call Jon. (972) 555-2455.

We called Jon and found out that his wife had multiple sclerosis. They had a two-story home, and Jon's wife could no longer climb the stairs. They were selling because they needed a one-story home and needed money for medical bills. This was an abandoned property waiting to happen.

8. *Death*

"Death forces sale." This was the heading of a classified ad we read one morning in our local newspaper. This was a pretty tough situation, but the widow needed to sell after her husband was killed in a traffic accident.

9. Owner Will Carry

When you see or hear *owner will carry*, you have found a built-in real estate lender to finance the deal. The property owner is going to act as the lender. They are going to carry a mortgage or trust deed for part or the entire purchase price.

We have found that a property owner in distress will offer to carry financing in order to make their property more attractive to more buyers. We ask abandoned-property owners to carry the financing on property that we want to keep for long-term wealth building.

10. Nothing Down

No down payment. Zero. Nada. *Nothing down* means a property owner wants their property to be the most competitive one on the market. This can also be an indication that the property owner does not have a lot of time because of an impending foreclosure.

11. 100 Percent Financing

A variation of nothing down is *100 percent financing*. We may have a distressed property owner who has to sell his or her property and is willing to finance the sale rather than lose all their equity. This is one of those phrases that we never pass up when we encounter it.

12. Motivated Seller

A *motivated seller* is a motivated property owner. As a real estate investor you are looking for motivated sellers. Property owners in preforeclosure are motivated sellers. A motivated seller might just give you the deed to their property and walk away!

13. Lost Job or Laid Off

The color pink is an anachronism from the twentieth century when people actually got a pink slip to let them know that they were either fired or laid off. In the twenty-first-century economy, companies want fewer workers doing more work.

Foreclosure

A huge source of property owners in distress is in the foreclosure arena. For some of you, your access to abandoned-property investing will be through the foreclosure market.

We will present information on discovering property and property owners in foreclosure in the rest of this chapter. For a complete discussion of foreclosure, see our book *Quick Cash in Foreclosures* (John Wiley & Sons, 2004).

Advertise

Sometimes a well-placed advertisement in the newspaper, on the Internet, or notices posted on public bulletin boards in supermarkets or business establishments can place a property owner in distress in contact with you. We have had continuing success with the following wording as a newspaper, bulletin board, or Internet ad:

MISSED YOUR PAYMENT AGAIN?

Private party will share ways to save
your home/protect your equity.
Learn 8 ways to avoid foreclosure.
Free! Call (817) 555-1212.

Searching the Public Record

There are two ways to search the public record to glean information about foreclosures or potential foreclosures. You can do it yourself, or you can pay a foreclosure service to provide you with the foreclosure information.

Do It Yourself

For most of you, the public records are at your local county courthouse. For some of you, the public records may be at your city hall. More and more, you can access the public records through the Internet.

The problem with checking the public records yourself is the tremendous number of records there are to check. That's why title insurance companies have to do a title search on a property before they will issue title insurance. This process can take several weeks. The title insurance company will issue a preliminary title report as a prelude to issuing a policy of title insurance.

We recommend you plan on making a day of it to visit the county recorder's office for your county. You will probably find the public records section buried deep in the bowels of your county courthouse.

Ask for Help

Ask for help from the staff to direct you to the foreclosure postings for the current month. Once you have the legal description of the property from the foreclosure posting and the property owner's name, you can look up the property in the public record and also check for liens against the owner.

The property record will reflect any liens against the property owner. If you are going to do business with a new buyer, you might also want to check them out. For example, if you are going to flip a foreclosure property and carry back financing, this would be a good idea. Sometimes the new buyer will bring clouds to the property title because of liens associated with them personally, like IRS liens.

Foreclosure Service

You can get information about foreclosures from a foreclosure service. A typical price may be $35 per month for the foreclosure list for your county. A typical price for the year may be $225.

Shop around because there may be more than one foreclosure service in your area. You don't need anything fancy; just the basic information will do.

Foreclosure Letter

For some of you, face-to-face contact with strangers on a subject of such a sensitive nature as foreclosure may prove uncomfortable. Also, it may be tough for a property owner facing foreclosure to come to grips with their shame and embarrassment. For both of these reasons, a letter campaign may be a good method to consider in your pursuit of eligible properties.

Although nothing beats personal contact, a program of contacting property owners in distress via mail is often the only way to reach an owner who is difficult to find. They may be occupying the property but have an unlisted or disconnected telephone number. They may have vacated the property but left a forwarding address. Just as in the personal contact and telephone meetings, your letter should be honest, sincere, and offer the property owner hope.

In addition to the letter, we want you to include a picture of the property, which will create a greater impact for the owner. The picture will show the owner that you have a strong interest in the property. After all, you came out to look at the property to take the picture! Make sure you keep a copy of the picture for your files should the property owner contact you at a later date.

The following is the letter we have used. You may want to consider using it. You can change it to fit your style and needs. You will notice that this letter is not a short and sweet letter. It is a short and to-the-point letter. The purpose of your letter is to get the property owner's attention. The purpose of your letter is also to have the property owner contact you because they feel you can help them.

Dear Property Owner,

According to the public records, the loan on your property may be in trouble. We are writing to you with an offer to help. We are real estate investors who have studied the foreclosure process. We are familiar with the procedure and understand the many ways in which an owner can halt the foreclosure and perhaps save his property and equity.

We have made it a practice to contact owners like you who have received official notice of a pending foreclosure. We believe we may be able to help you by providing information about your foreclosure options. Sometimes we find excellent investment opportunities when owners have decided that they no longer wish to keep their property.

Specifically, there are eight actions you can take when your home is in foreclosure. We would like to share these options with you *at no cost or obligation to you.* We do this to increase our chances for investment opportunities and at the same time to have an opportunity to help some owners who would otherwise lose their properties.

Time is running out! We urge you to contact us today before any more of your hard-earned equity is lost forever. We can be reached by phone, e-mail, or letter. We will keep our conversation confidential. Hopefully, we can provide you with the information you need to save your property. **DON'T WAIT!** Contact us today!

Chantal and Bill Carey

VA and FHA Foreclosures

You can find out about Veterans Administration (VA) and Federal Housing Administration (FHA) foreclosures from your local VA and HUD (Department of Housing and Urban Development) offices. They will likely refer you to a list of VA- and FHA-approved real estate brokers in your area who are authorized to list and give access to VA and FHA real estate owned (REO) portfolios.

These properties are auctioned off to the highest net bidder. The highest net bidder is the bidder whose bid after real estate commissions and expenses generates the most cash to the VA or FHA. Incidentally, your bid must be submitted in writing through an approved real estate broker. These are sealed bids that are opened by the appropriate VA or FHA representatives on a designated date.

Federal National Mortgage Association/Fannie Mae
Fannie Mae is a stockholder-owned, congressionally chartered corporation. Its stock is traded on the New York Stock Exchange and other major exchanges. It is listed on the Standard and Poor's 500 Stock Price Index. By buying and selling VA, FHA, and conventional loans in the secondary mortgage market, Fannie Mae is the largest real estate lender in the country.

Fannie Mae Foreclosures
As the largest real estate lender, Fannie Mae has its share of foreclosures. As a stock corporation, it is profit oriented and interested in minimizing losses if possible. One method of doing so is the Fannie Mae Preforeclosure Sale program.

The result to real estate investors can be the purchase of property from potential borrowers in default at prices below the existing loan and with new loan terms better than terms available on the open market. This is done on a case-by-case basis.

Why would Fannie Mae be willing to do this? The answer is to minimize losses. It is expensive for Fannie Mae to foreclose on, maintain, and then remarket a portfolio of properties. If it can dispose of the properties in preforeclosure, before it takes them into its property portfolio, Fannie Mae can save money.

The program is directed toward real estate agents as the contact source with defaulting borrowers, potential retail or wholesale buyers, and the lenders, including Fannie Mae. Just as with VA and FHA foreclosures, you must discover who are the real estate brokers handling Fannie Mae properties. Whether Fannie Mae moves to a new program, they will always be a source of foreclosure opportunities. Once you have established contact with a Fannie Mae broker, they will be able to keep you informed on any changes.

Your entry into the abandoned-property market can be through the abandoned-property owners or the abandoned property itself. Our discussion about motivated property owners has overlapped abandoned property. In the next chapter, we will show you how to find abandoned property. There are 10 clues to look for to find abandoned property.

CHAPTER 4

How to Find Abandoned Property

Finding a good deal is the key to your success in real estate. Every deal has the potential to be a good deal. This is especially the case with abandoned-property deals. As every real estate investor will tell you, you want to buy low and sell high. Although this is easily said, it is sometimes hard to do.

It is hard to do for different reasons than most people would think. The reasons are not because of the nature of the real estate market. The reasons it is hard for most people to buy low and sell high and easy for people to buy high and sell low are psychological.

Before you can find a good abandoned-property deal, you must understand the psychology of the real estate market. Once you understand the psychology of the real estate market, you can move forward without fear that you are going to make a mistake. The biggest mistake you can make is failing to start real estate investing.

After you have overcome the psychological barrier to becoming a successful real estate investor, finding a good abandoned-property deal is easy. We will show you the six ways to find a good deal. Then we will give you our 10 clues to look for to find abandoned property.

The Psychology of Markets

Every market has a psychology that shapes it. For example, in the stock market two emotions shape the market. These two emotions are fear and greed. People get into the stock market based on fear and greed. They get a hot stock tip from a friend or someone at work or from someone who knows someone.

This is when fear and greed take over. They are afraid of missing out by not acting on the tip, and they get greedy by investing before they conduct a due-diligence investigation. In other words, they fail to determine value. People don't realize that the best stock deals are the ones they discover for themselves. Besides, by the time they get a hot stock tip, it is too late.

The smart investors are already selling to the people who are buying because of the tip. The smart investors bought low and are now selling high. Most people are buying high and then wind up selling low when the stock or the market itself moves lower.

The Psychology of the Real Estate Market

The real estate market has four times the assets of the stock market! The truth be told, however, there is no real estate market. There are only people to talk to. We say it this way: *Contacts create contracts.* Contact with people creates opportunity for you as a real estate investor. To be a successful real estate investor, you must talk to people.

The psychology of the real estate market is shaped by four emotions. These four emotions are the fear and greed of the stock market plus the emotions of pride of ownership and shyness.

Fear and Greed

We have never been caught up in the fear and greed of the real estate market. There is no deal so good that you have to jump on it or it will disappear. If a real estate deal sounds too good to be true, that is because it *is* too good to be true. This is especially true with abandoned-property deals. There is no scarcity of good abandoned-property deals.

As with every successful real estate investor, you will do your due diligence before investing. This means you will know value in your target area. You will build in profit by how you write your offer. Then you will be buying low or will not be buying at all! After all, you can't sell high unless you bought low!

Pride of Ownership

Every property owner suffers from pride of ownership. As a real estate investor, you do not suffer the emotion of pride of ownership. If you do, it becomes an expensive emotion to entertain.

Homeowners tend to overvalue their property because they have lived in the property, perhaps raised a family in the property, and made improvements to the property. When it comes time to sell their property, homeowners tend to inflate the value of their home because of the pride they feel in their home.

Corporate property owners also have a pride of ownership. After all, it is *their* building, or tower, or landmark. In fact, it has been our experience that some corporate property owners can overvalue their property to an even greater extent than a residential property owner.

A real estate investor takes pride of ownership into account when they are negotiating with a homeowner or any property owner. Pride of ownership, however, does not figure into an objective valuation of property for the real estate investor. It has been amazing to us the number of abandoned-property owners we have encountered who still cling to the pride of ownership emotion even after they have abandoned the property!

Be Bold!

The number one psychological emotion or barrier a real estate investor must overcome is shyness. You may not be shy when it comes to finding abandoned property, locating abandoned-property owners, or writing an abandoned-property offer. Most beginning and even some veteran real estate investors become shy when it comes to presenting the abandoned-property offer. *Don't be shy. Be bold!*

Six Ways to Find a Good Abandoned-Property Deal

There are six ways to find a good abandoned-property deal. They include checking classified ads either in newspapers or on the Internet, placing your newspaper or Internet ad, enlisting the help of personal contacts, doing your own scouting, visiting open houses, and working with a real estate agent.

1. Classified Ads

Checking classified ads either in newspapers or on the Internet is the first of six ways to find a good abandoned-property deal. The Friday and Sunday metropolitan editions are the best sources to find the most comprehensive real estate ads. Normally, you start looking in the existing property for sale sections.

With the cooling of the new-home market, we recommend you also look in the new homes for sale section. We predict that you will find some great abandoned-property deals from new-home builders who are stuck with unsold inventory.

Also look in the residential income real estate section and land, industrial, or commercial real estate. Remember to start in your target area first and expand outward from there (our stone in the pond idea).

Online
Most of the major metropolitan newspapers have their classified real estate ads available online. If you are a paperless person, this may be your best source to find abandoned property without leaving the comfort of your computer. We use the Internet but prefer the look and feel of scouting our target area.

The National Association of Realtors (www.realtor.org) and local real estate multiple listing services allow the public to visit their web sites and peruse available real estate company listings. Discount brokers like BuyOwner.com post properties with which they are assisting sellers. For-sale-by-owner sites like propertySites.com give you access to local for-sale-by-owner properties.

2. Placing Your Own Newspaper or Internet Ad

Placing your own newspaper or Internet ad is the second way to find a good abandoned-property deal. Place your ad in the real estate wanted section of the classified ads. It can be something simple and short:

Real Estate Investor buying property
in your area this week only!
Cash! Call (800) 555-1212.

You can place an Internet ad in your metropolitan newspaper. You can also place Internet ads on local and national Internet sites. We recommend you place local Internet ads that will have an impact on property owners in your target area.

3. Personal Contacts

Enlisting the help of personal contacts is the third way to find a good abandoned-property deal. Tell your family and friends you are investing in real estate. Let people at work, at church, and at social groups know that you are a real estate investor. Tell them that if they bring you a good deal that works out, you will pay them a referral fee.

You may learn about an impending divorce. You may hear about an illness. Someone may have recently died in an accident. You may hear about an upcoming plant closing. There is the gossip of a scandal at city hall.

You may find a money partner or real estate investor partner once you start talking to people. A good real estate agent may come your way. You may make contact with a good loan officer, escrow agent, or real estate attorney. As we said earlier in this chapter: *Don't be shy. Be bold!*

4. Scouting

Doing your own scouting is the fourth way to find a good abandoned-property deal. Driving your target area a different way each day can lead you to a good deal. Use side streets rather than thoroughfares. Take an extra 15 minutes driving home from work to look at property. Shop at a different grocery store. Drive through unfamiliar neighborhoods.

Scouting is our favorite way to find abandoned property. Of the abandoned-property deals we have been involved with, more than half have been as a direct result of doing our own scouting. Over time, you will develop your own favorite way to find abandoned property.

Look at bulletin boards in stores and Laundromats for ads regarding real estate for sale. Put up a real estate investor flyer in the lunch room at work. Talk to people with whom you do business, such as the dry cleaner, shoe repairman, cable guy, plumber, and let them know you are a real estate investor looking for property.

5. Open Houses

Visiting open houses is the fifth way to find an abandoned-property deal. Make it a point to drive around your target area on Saturday or Sunday and stop at real estate company and for-sale-by-owner open houses. Pick up the flyer about the property from the outside signage or ask for one when you tour the property. An open house in a vacant home may be a step away from an abandoned property.

Ask questions of the real estate agent or seller holding the open house. Inform them you are a real estate investor. Tell them you are prepared to make them an offer today if the property fits your parameters.

If you are visiting a property hosted by a real estate agent, the real estate agent will ask you questions in an attempt to get you to agree to work with the agent. Agree to nothing until you read the next section!

6. Real Estate Agents

Working with a real estate agent is the sixth way to find an abandoned-property deal. When you call about classified ads placed by real estate companies, you can begin to search for a real estate agent with whom you can feel comfortable working. Although just about every real estate agent works for the property owner, the only way the real estate agent makes any money is when there is a buyer who buys their seller's property.

You can get the real estate agent on your side by having them make money. When you close your first deal, they will then know you are a serious buyer. You are the best kind of buyer because you are a real estate investor.

Rather than making only one real estate purchase every five to seven years, like most retail buyers make for a home purchase, you are going to buy multiple real estate purchases in the course of one year. That means the real estate agent is going to make multiple real estate commissions.

When this agent knows your real estate investment parameters, they will actively seek properties for you. The real estate agent can now legitimately go to a property owner and say that the agent has a buyer for their property. Real estate agents can be a great source of abandoned property.

However, caveat emptor—let the buyer beware—is a good place to start when you approach a real estate agent. Just as it may take you a while to find a good abandoned-property deal, it may take you a while to find a good real estate agent.

The 10 Clues to Look For to Find Abandoned Property

There are 10 clues to look for to find abandoned property. These 10 clues correspond to elements that come under the

four great forces that influence value. Remember the four great
forces that influence value are physical forces, economic forces,
political forces, and social forces. Each of these four great forces
includes elements that can have a positive upward influence or
a negative downward influence on real estate value.

The 10 clues to look for are elements of the great forces
that, if they are present, can have a negative downward influence on value in your target area. The rule of thumb in
abandoned-property investing is that if property value is going
down, the amount of abandoned property is going up. By looking for these 10 clues, you can get a very good sense of whether
abandoned property will be found in your target area.

Initially, it would seem that if you find four, five, or six
clues it would imply a preponderance of elements that will
have a negative downward influence on real estate value. This
would seem to indicate the potential for more abandoned
property. Although we have found this is the case, this is not a
majority-rules situation.

It has been our experience that it is possible to find only
one clue and find many abandoned properties in a target area.
For example, if there is an economic depression that affects
your target area, there will be many abandoned properties. On
the other hand, it is also possible to find nine clues and find
very few abandoned properties!

1. Schools, Shopping, Churches, Transportation, and Parks

Physical forces are the first of the great forces that influence
the value of real estate. The availability of schools, shopping,
churches, transportation, and parks are physical forces that
influence real estate value. If these physical amenities are present in your target area, they influence the value of the area in
an upward manner. If these physical amenities are not present
or are minimally present in your target area, they influence the
value of the area in a downward manner.

Clue one is looking for schools, shopping, churches, public
transportation, and parks in your target area. If they are not present or are minimally present or are regarded as poor in quality, it
is a clue that you will be able to find abandoned property.

We will give you one caveat. In new areas of growth, many houses can be built in the middle of nowhere. There may be no schools, shopping, churches, public transportation, or parks in the area, but there is no abandoned property, either.

2. Economic Cycle

The economic cycle is a repeating expansion, prosperity, recession, depression cycle. Real estate value is greatly influenced by the economic cycle. Typically, real estate is said to do well in the expansion and prosperity phases of the economic cycle. Real estate is said to do poorly in the recession and depression phases of the economic cycle.

Clue two is seeing where in the economic cycle we are. If we are in the recession phase or the depression phase of the economic cycle, this is a strong clue that you will be able to find abandoned property. In today's political climate, recession is the politically correct way to say depression.

This is a huge opportunity to make money. You must overcome the mass psychology that will be prevalent in the media and publicly that real estate is a bad investment. This is when you can find abandoned property and buy it for a low or wholesale price.

3. Interest Rates

The interest rates for real estate loans are economic forces that influence real estate value. If the interest rates are relatively low historically, it has a positive influence on real estate values. If the interest rates are relatively high historically, it has a negative influence on real estate values.

Clue three is checking real estate interest rates. High interest rates are a clue that you will be able to find abandoned property. There is a direct correlation between rising interest rates and increasing foreclosure rates. The higher the foreclosure rate in your target area, the more abandoned properties you will find.

4. Wages to Be Paid

The wages paid in an area have an impact on the value of real estate. High wages—in other words, good-paying jobs—have an upward impact on real estate values. Low wages have a downward impact on real estate values.

Clue four is checking wage rates in your target area. Low wage rates are a clue that you will be able to find abandoned property. People are not making enough money to support either the businesses in the area or the property-tax base in the area. Business property and commercial property may then have a greater likelihood of being abandoned.

5. Manufacturing Plant and Military Base Closings

Manufacturing plant closures and military base closures will have huge negative economic impacts on an area. This translates almost immediately to a downward impact on real estate values. Government military base closings and automotive and manufacturing plant shutdowns will occur with unpleasant regularity over the next 36 months.

Clue five is being aware of upcoming manufacturing plant or military base closings in your target area. Loss of jobs is one of the financial reasons why property owners abandon their property. Manufacturing plant and military base closings mean loss of jobs. This will translate into many abandoned properties.

6. Zoning

The types of zoning are political forces that influence the value of real estate. The types of zoning will have an impact on the present real estate investment climate and the future real estate investment climate.

Clue six is being aware of zoning changes in your target area. Increasing zoning density tends to increase the value of property. Decreasing zoning density tends to decrease the value of property. Decreasing zoning density can mean an increase in abandoned property.

Brain Trust

A Brain Trust idea is for you to become a member of your local planning commission or zoning commission. Then you will have firsthand knowledge and a say-so in decisions that will affect the value of property in your target area.

This will also apply to clue eight, pro-growth or no growth. By your involvement in the planning and zoning arena, you can have a positive impact on continued growth in your area. Pro-growth means increasing property values. No growth means decreasing property values.

7. Environmental Impacts

Environmental impacts can have a huge affect on the value of real estate. New Orleans and the Gulf Coast are still recovering from the effects of Hurricane Katrina in August 2005. Toxic waste that affects the ground, water, and air can turn real estate values upside down.

Clue seven is determining first if your target area itself has potential environmental impacts. Then determine if a particular property may have a problem. An environmental impact can be property specific, such as the presence of asbestos, that can drive down the property value and lead to the property being abandoned.

8. Pro-growth or No Growth

Progrowth political forces have a positive impact on real estate values. No-growth political forces have a negative impact on real estate values. Your target area will be affected by which one of these political forces is currently in vogue.

Clue eight is discovering which way the political progrowth or no-growth winds are blowing. There may be many abandoned properties in your target area if there has been a prolonged period of no-growth political forces.

9. Blighted Neighborhoods

Blighted neighborhoods are a social force that influences the value of real estate in a downward direction. Good neighborhoods are a social force that influences the value of real estate in an upward direction.

Clue nine is discovering if there are any blighted neighborhoods in your target area. Usually we think of a blighted neighborhood as a residential area. A blighted neighborhood could also be a commercial or industrial area. A blighted neighborhood contains abandoned property.

10. Racial or Ethnic Strife

Racial or ethnic strife is also a social force that influences the value of real estate in a downward direction. Lack of racial or ethnic strife in an area influences the value of real estate in an upward direction.

Clue 10 is being aware of potential or actual racial or ethnic strife in your target area. As a new racial or ethnic group moves into an area, the existing racial or ethnic group may move out of that area. During this transition, there may be an increase in abandoned property.

Taken as an aggregate, these 10 clues make it is easy to see where an increased supply of abandoned property will come from over the next 36 months. Factor in a downturn in the overall economy. Add in rising interest rates. We continue to export high-paying jobs. We will have manufacturing plant and military base closures. This will lead to more foreclosures.

The number of blighted neighborhoods will increase. Racial and ethnic strife will continue to rear its ugly head. Zoning changes, including eminent-domain taking of private property for public use, will restrict property use. No-growth policies and negative environmental impacts will depress the value of real estate. Lack of infrastructure or decaying infrastructure will reduce the quality of life.

The silver lining in these clouds is that although the number of abandoned properties will increase, we as abandoned-property real estate investors will be able to have a positive impact on restoring value to our target areas around the country. We will be the people rehabilitating these abandoned properties. Of course, because we are taking the risks, we are entitled to make money investing in abandoned property.

Once you have found an abandoned property, you must locate the abandoned-property owner. In the next chapter, we will show you how to locate owners who have abandoned their property. There are five ways to locate these abandoned-property owners. Before you write your abandoned-property offer, you must figure out to whom, where, and how you are going to present your offer.

CHAPTER 5

How to Locate Owners Who Have Abandoned Their Property

There are five ways to locate an owner who has abandoned his or her property. It can be as lucky as finding the owner at the property. It may be a simple as calling the number on the for-sale sign or using a reverse directory and discovering the property owner's phone number. It can involve checking with the local property-taxing authority to find out who is responsible for paying the property taxes.

You may have to do some research and look up ownership, deed, and lien records. Finally, you may have to file legal action in the form of an abandonment of property lawsuit or a foreclosure action to get the abandoned-property owner to make contact with you.

Five Ways to Locate an Owner Who Has Abandoned A Property

You must find the owner who has abandoned a property in order to present your offer. You need the property owner's signature on your offer in order to create a deal. Then you need their signature on escrow instructions and ownership deeds.

In general, it is more difficult to buy property and get the title to the property without the property owner's signature; however, this can be done. We will give you the particulars as we go through this chapter. Let's start with the easy way to do an abandoned-property deal and find the property owner.

1. Find the Owner at the Property

We like the expression "I'd rather be lucky than good." Actually, we prefer to be lucky *and* good. The first way to locate owners who have abandoned their property is to find them at the property. We have found the abandoned-property owner at the property many times. It may be our good luck. It may be that we are really good at being persistent.

Normally, an abandoned property is vacant. Anytime we see a moving van or people in the process of moving, we stop and start asking questions. We introduce ourselves as real estate investors. We ask where they are moving. We ask them what they are going to do with the property. We always ask them if they would be interested in selling the property.

Once we have determined a property is vacant, we drive by it every chance we get. We vary the times to increase the likelihood that we may find someone at the property. We even recommend you drive by at night. If the owners work during the day, their only opportunity to check on the property or remove any remaining belongings will be at night.

Fannie Mae

One day we drove by a property that we knew was vacant. We saw a car in the driveway. We stopped and rang the doorbell. It turned out that the person who answered the door was an appraiser. Fannie Mae, the Federal National Mortgage Association, had taken back the property at a foreclosure sale.

The appraiser was at the property taking measurements and doing an appraisal for Fannie Mae. We told the appraiser we were real estate investors. We asked the appraiser if we could come in and look around. He said yes, and we went in.

Brain Trust

Anytime you have an opportunity to talk with an appraiser who is in the field making an appraisal, do it. By building rapport with the appraiser, you can glean valuable information not only about the property he or she is appraising but also about the real estate market in your target area.

We found out from the appraiser that Fannie Mae was going to rehab the property with new paint and floor coverings. Fannie Mae was then going to list the property with a real estate broker. The appraiser was going to do his appraisal based on what the market value of the property would be after it was rehabbed.

The appraiser also told us that he was going to be doing a bunch of appraisals in our target area for Fannie Mae about these market value of the property after rehabbing. He also felt that the real estate market was slowing for residential resales, and in some areas prices were actually dropping.

This was an abandoned-property deal waiting to happen! We contacted Fannie Mae and told them we wanted to buy the property. We didn't want them to do the rehab. We didn't want them to list the property with a real estate broker.

We would buy the property directly from Fannie Mae and save them and us the rehab expenses and the real estate commissions.

We found out that Fannie Mae was going to put the property on the market for $179,900. We made them an all-cash offer for $155,000. Fannie Mae accepted our offer. This saved us $24,900 off the top.

Fannie Mae accepted our offer because they would have accepted $175,000, paid a 6 percent real estate commission, had $5,500 in rehab costs in the property, and had to wait three, four, five, or six months to receive an offer from a qualified retail buyer. The possibility for Fannie Mae to make an additional $3,000 or $4,000 was not worth them holding onto this property when they had us as a cash buyer and a bunch more properties coming into their real estate owned portfolio.

Our Offer to Fannie Mae

Fannie Mae List Price	$179,900
Our Offer to Fannie Mae	−$155,000
Savings to Us	$24,900

Fannie Mae Sells to a Retail Buyer

Fannie Mae Sales Price	$175,000
Real Estate Commissions	10,500
Fannie Mae Rehab Costs	−$5,500
Fannie Mae Nets	$159,000
Our Offer to Fannie Mae	−$155,000
Difference to Fannie Mae	$4,000

Make Money

During the closing period, we assigned our contract with Fannie Mae to a cash buyer for $162,000. We received a $7,000 assignment fee from the buyer. The buyer then paid Fannie Mae $155,000 at the closing.

Make Money

Sold For	$162,000
Fannie Mae Received	−$155,000
Our Assignment Fee	$7,000

2. Call the Number on the Sign or Use a Reverse Directory

The second way to locate owners who have abandoned their property is to call the number on the for-sale sign or use a reverse directory. Sometimes an abandoned property has an existing for-sale sign. We start with calling the number on the for-sale sign. You may actually reach the abandoned-property owner. Identify yourself as a real estate investor and ask if they are interested in selling the property.

The purpose of our call is to make an appointment with the owners to see their property. In one case, when the owners arrived we discovered they had moved out of the property six months ago. They had tried to rent the property but had been unsuccessful.

The owners were too busy at their work and lived too far away to spend the necessary time to successfully market their property. They were desperate for a solution. They were on the verge of just walking away from the property completely. This was an abandoned property waiting to happen!

We determined the property was worth $195,000 to $205,000, depending on its condition. The owners had a mortgage of $157,000. They were trying to sell the property for $175,000. The owners told us that if they could get $5,000 cash, they would sell us the property! For $5,000 we would have a $43,000 equity position in the property!

Our Equity

Property Value	$200,000
Mortgage	−$157,000
Our Equity	$43,000

With abandoned property, however, you must investigate a bit further. We told the owners we were interested in buying their property. We wanted to do some research before we made them an offer.

We discovered that the loan payments were current and were $1,200 per month. The property taxes were current, but six months of property taxes were accumulated and amounted to $2,500. We inspected the property and realized we would have to replace the carpeting. This would cost $4,000.

We went back to the owners and said we would buy their property under the following conditions. We would give them their requested $5,000. If we were going to give them $5,000, however, we wanted them to compensate us $4,000 for the carpeting, $2,500 for the six months of the property taxes that was their responsibility, and $3,600 for the next three mortgage payments.

We explained to the owners that they would be responsible for three mortgage payments if we had a 90-day closing. If they agreed to our offer, we would close in three days. How did the deal look now?

Owner Pays

Owner Pays Carpeting	$4,000
Owner Pays Taxes	$2,500
Owner Pays Three Monthly Payments	+$3,600
Total	$10,100

Buyer Receives at Closing

Owner Pays	$10,100
Buyer Credits Owner	−$5,000
Buyer Receives at Closing	$5,100

Why did the owners agree to our offer? Because they had already abandoned the property. They had moved out. They wanted to be free of the property. It was just a matter of a relatively short period of time before they would have stopped making the mortgage payments and gone into foreclosure.

The owners paid us $5,100 to make their abandoned property problem go away. We now had a $43,000 equity position in the property. We had $5,100 cash in our pockets.

Reverse Directory

A reverse directory is a very useful tool if you are investing in the abandoned-property business. A reverse directory will give you the property owner's name and phone number if you have the address of the property. A reverse directory will also give you the address of the property if you have the owner's name and telephone number.

Check out www.ReversePhoneDirectory.com. This is a reverse-lookup directory, including reverse-phone-number search and address lookup for people and businesses. It also gives regions corresponding to area and ZIP codes.

In the interests of completeness and simplicity, you could look up the property owner's name in the phone book. There is also the option of calling information.

U.S. Mail

Sometimes a simple but effective way to locate the abandoned-property owner is to send them a letter. Once you have discovered the name of the property owner, start out by sending them a letter to the property address. With any luck, it will be forwarded to a good address for the property owner.

If the letter does not come back or if you receive no response from the property owner, send them a certified letter with return receipt requested. If you get confirmation of delivery, then you know the property owner received your letter. Again, if you get no response, you can try again or see if you can get better contact information.

3. Check with the Local Property-Taxing Authority

The third way to locate owners who have abandoned their property is to check on the Internet the property-tax information for your target area. Property taxes in the United States are controlled by local county tax assessors and collectors. Typically, they will have a web site. If not, you may also appear in person and gain access to the property-tax records because they are a matter of public record.

An abandoned property is still subject to property taxes. By using the property-tax ownership information, you may be able to locate the property owner. The tax billing address may be different from the property address.

Once you have the tax billing address, use the reverse directory to see if you can find a phone number for the property owner. If you can't find a phone number, send the property owner a letter or a certified letter with return receipt requested at the property tax billing address.

You may discover looking at the property-tax records that the property taxes are delinquent or haven't been paid. This may give you another opportunity to make money with this abandoned property.

Real Estate Tax Liens
Sooner or later, the property-taxing authority will either sell the property for back property taxes or sell a tax lien certificate. See our book *Make Money in Real Estate Tax Liens*

(John Wiley & Sons, 2005) for a complete discussion about investing in real estate tax liens in your area.

You may find that the taxing authority has already conducted a tax lien sale. Don't despair! There are three opportunities to buy tax liens after the tax lien sale. This is a way to control abandoned property without making a deal with the abandoned-property owner!

The first opportunity is called over-the-counter buying. The second opportunity is buying the tax lien through the mail. The third opportunity is contacting the winning bidder after the tax lien sale and making them an offer they cannot refuse.

1. Over-the-Counter Buying

The first opportunity to buy tax liens after the tax lien sale is if the tax liens offered for sale at the tax sale draw no interested buyers. In these cases, the tax liens revert to the county or appropriate taxing authority. The taxing authority then will be the holder of these tax liens.

The taxing authority will make the tax liens available to investors after the sale. No competitive bid will be required. When you buy tax liens from the taxing authority after the taxing authority has unsuccessfully attempted to auction them, this is called over-the-counter buying.

The procedures for over-the-counter buying vary by area. You must check with the taxing authority to find out when it accepts bids on these unsold tax liens. Sometimes, the taxing authority will accept bids anytime after the auction is over. Other times, bidding is restricted to certain time periods.

If your investment strategy is to acquire the property itself, it is even more important that you have seen the property. When a tax lien does not sell at the auction, it could be because there were not enough interested investors present. It could also be because the property is damaged or perhaps even worthless.

You must not make an over-the-counter purchase of a real estate tax lien that is worth more than the property. If you do, you have just thrown away your money. The abandoned-property owner is not going to redeem the tax lien. You will not be able to foreclose on your tax lien after the redemption period and sell the property for the amount of money you have invested in the tax lien.

2. Buying Tax Liens by Mail

The second opportunity to buy tax liens after the tax lien sale is if the taxing authorities accept tax lien investor offers by mail. You can verify the procedure for this with a phone call. If the property is located far from where you live, purchasing by mail is a great way to keep down your expenses.

The obvious pitfall to purchasing a tax lien by mail is that you will not have looked at the property. Only by researching the area and everything about the property in particular can you safely make this kind of a tax lien purchase.

We suggest you contact a local real estate broker to help you with your research. The broker can provide you market data information about the area. The broker can also run comps on the property that is the security for the tax lien.

You may be able to get this information for free. The broker may agree to help you in order to create goodwill and generate future business. If you must pay the real estate broker a small fee, it will well be worth it. You may even get them to drive by the property and send you pictures.

3. Buying from the Winning Bidder

The third opportunity to buy tax liens after the tax lien sale is if you contact the winning bidder and make them an offer they cannot refuse. They may take an immediate cash return on their investment rather than wait for the tax lien to be paid off. You would be willing to do this because you are going to be paid very handsomely to wait.

Let's say the winning bidder bought a tax lien for $4,000. You offer them $4,500. They make an immediate $500 profit in a relatively brief period of time.

Buying from the Winning Bidder

Winning Bidder Paid	$4,000
Your Offer	−$4,500
Their Profit	$500

How do you make a profit? Suppose the interest rate the taxing authority lawfully sets to pay you as the buyer of the tax lien certificate is 18 percent. What would your profit be over two years? Amazingly, you would have a 16 percent annual return on your $4,500 investment!

Your Profit

Tax Lien Certificate	$4,000
Annual Interest Rate	× 18%
First-Year Profit	$720
Second-Year Profit	×$720
Your Profit	$1,440

Annual Return

$1,440/$4,500	= 32%
32%/Two Years	= 16%

4. Look Up Ownership, Deed, and Lien Records

The fourth way to locate owners who have abandoned their property is to look up ownership, deed, and lien records. Again, in the United States the county is the record keeper for public records. Typically, they will have a web site. If not, you may also appear in person and gain access to the ownership, deed, and lien records at the county courthouse because they are a matter of public record.

You can also develop a relationship with a title insurance company and have them check ownership records. They may do this for free with the implied expectation that you will do title insurance business with them. Sometimes this is called a property profile. If you want a preliminary title report that shows ownership, deed, and lien information, you may be charged a fee.

You may discover that an abandoned-property owner's lender has foreclosed on the property. The lender is now the abandoned-property owner. What about buying the abandoned property from the lender after the foreclosure sale?

Usually, the lender has the biggest financial stake in the property. After all, they made an 80 percent, a 90 percent, a 95 percent, 97 percent, or even 100 percent loan to the borrower to buy the property to begin with. Can you get a good abandoned-property deal from the lender once the property goes out of the lender's loan portfolio and into the lender's property portfolio? We say the answer is yes.

Lender Real Estate Owned Portfolios

Lenders' property portfolios are called real estate owned portfolios, or REOs for short. Real estate lenders are in the business of making real estate loans. Real estate lenders are not in the business of owning real estate. Although the lender wants to sell their REOs for as much as possible, they also want to move these REO properties as quickly as possible.

We found an abandoned property that had been foreclosed on by the lender. When no one bid above the lender's credit bid of $93,527.23 at the foreclosure sale, the trustee awarded the lender a trustee's deed. The lender now owned the property.

The next day, we called our contact person at the lender. We asked what the REO department was going to sell the property for. He told us they were going to list the property with a real estate broker for $85,000. He also told us that the price was negotiable!

REO Offer

We made an offer of $70,000 in cash for the property. We didn't want to buy the property for $70,000. We wanted to control the property for $70,000. We were not interested in coming up with $70,000 cash. We would leave that to the investor to whom we assigned our contract.

We submitted our offer through our contact person in the REO department. Our offering price wasn't a big bone of contention. The lender simply countered at $80,000. We countered their counteroffer with $73,900, and they accepted.

Our Offer

Lender List Price	$85,000
Our Offer	$70,000
Lender Counteroffer	$80,000
Our Counteroffer	$73,900

However, the lender was unwilling to allow us to assign our contract. We felt we would be able to work out an acceptable price with another investor. If we couldn't get the lender to allow us to assign our contract, then we would have no deal.

The Unassignable Contract

It has been our experience that there is no such thing as an unassignable contract. And the toughest contracts to assign are the ones from lenders after they have foreclosed on a loan and are reselling a property.

Real estate owned (REO) properties are the source of some of our most profitable abandoned-property inventory. Lenders are just as hoodwinked as the rest of us, however, when it comes to listening to attorneys. They allow their attorneys to put the dumbest things in their REO contracts. Our position on any contract is that the purpose of the contract is to communicate.

Real estate attorneys, just like other attorneys, make money by keeping people from communicating. The following is actual verbiage taken from the lender's REO contract that their attorneys put in:

REO REAL ESTATE CONTRACT

Buyer shall neither assign its rights nor delegate its obligations hereunder without obtaining Seller's prior written consent, which may be withheld in Seller's sole discretion. In no event shall an assignment relieve Buyer from its obligations under this Contract. Any other purported or attempted assignment or delegation without obtaining Seller's prior written consent shall be void and of no effect.

Needless to say, this paragraph was unacceptable to us. How did we get around this affront to our investor sensibilities? Did we get the lender's prior written consent before we wrote an offer? No, we did not. Our contact person gave us a clue.

We wrote the offer as trustees of a trust. As such, we were speaking the language the lender could understand. We did not know when we wrote the offer which trust was actually going to buy the property. The lender accepted our offer as Chantal Carey or Bill Carey, Trustees and/or assigns. We assigned the lender's unassignable contract within seven days after our offer was accepted for $6,000.

Our Profit

Sale Price	$79,900
Purchase Price	−$73,900
Our Profit	$6,000

We must say here that dealing with REO lenders and their attorneys is very difficult. You must legitimately be a trustee before you can write and present contracts as one. We do not recommend this technique if you are just starting out in the abandoned-property foreclosure business.

For those of you who are more advanced or are trustees of trusts and want to consult with us for more information, contact us through our e-mail address, thetrustee@hotmail. com. You must fully identify yourself, or we will not open the e-mail nor respond to it.

5. File Legal Action

The fifth way to locate owners who have abandoned their property is to file legal action. This could be in the form of a foreclosure action or an abandonment of property lawsuit to get the abandoned-property owner to make contact with you.

This may be a last resort to locate the abandoned-property owner when all your other efforts have failed. We have heard of some abandoned-property investors who have hired a private detective to locate the abandoned-property owner. We feel that is unnecessary. Try what we recommend in this section first.

Foreclosure Action

Besides buying an abandoned property from a foreclosing lender's REO department, we have another way to locate owners who have abandoned their property. Buy a mortgage on the property from a lender of record. The mortgage may or may not be in default. If the property is abandoned, it will be only a matter of time before the mortgage or mortgages will be in default.

Your first step is to look up what mortgages are liens against the title to the property. Mortgages are recorded in the public record. Contact the mortgage holders through the information you obtain from your search of the public records.

Let them know you are a real estate investor who is interested in buying their mortgage paper. This is easier to do if the mortgage holder is a private individual. Typically, this would be the previous owner who extended a mortgage to the current abandoned-property owner when they bought the property.

If the only mortgage(s) on the property is held by institutional lenders, you may have a more difficult time tracking down who actually holds the mortgage paper. Usually, there is a servicing lender who collects the mortgage payments from the borrower for a third-party mortgage holder like Fannie Mae or Freddie Mac.

Your real intent here is to get information on the location of or contact information for the abandoned-property owner from the institutional or private mortgage holder. After all, you are interested in buying or controlling the property. We have found it easier to get this information from private mortgage holders because of the privacy laws that institutional lenders must follow.

By pursuing the information as a potential mortgage-loan purchaser, we have been able to find out the status of the loan. After all, investors prefer buying good mortgage paper rather than bad mortgage paper. Good mortgage paper has payments that are current. Bad mortgage paper has payments that are in arrears.

If you do wind up buying the mortgage paper, you have several options. Because you bought the mortgage paper at a discount, if the borrower/abandoned-property owner continues to make payments, you have made a good investment. (For a complete discussion of buying mortgages at a discount, see our book *The New Path to Real Estate Wealth* [John Wiley & Sons, 2003].) You should now have location or contact information for the abandoned-property owner.

If they get behind on their mortgage payments, however, you can file a notice of default and begin foreclosure proceedings. If they do not correct the mortgage default, you foreclose on your mortgage and get title to the property, or you can make a deal with them to buy the property before the foreclosure sale goes through.

Abandonment of Property Lawsuit

As a last resort, you can file an abandonment of property lawsuit to see if you can get the abandoned-property owner to make contact. This is called a quiet title action. You are attempting to get a court to extinguish or quiet the title of the abandoned-property owner in the property. Your success in getting the court to grant you title is dependent on local law and custom. We have never done this.

Now that you have located the abandoned-property owner, the next step is to write your abandoned-property offer. In the next chapter, we will show you how to write a foolproof abandoned-property offer. There are five requirements that must be included in your foolproof abandoned-property offer.

CHAPTER 6

How to Write a Foolproof Abandoned-Property Offer

There are no oral agreements in real estate. Everything must be in writing. In this chapter we will show you how to write an offer that will get you a great abandoned-property deal and at the same time protect you from winding up in a lousy deal. In the next chapter we will show you how to present your abandoned-property offer to the property owner in such a way that the abandoned-property owner will see the advantage in accepting your offer.

Writing Your Abandoned-Property Offer

As we have said, there are no oral agreements in real estate. Yes, technically, you can agree to buy someone's abandoned property and they can agree to sell it to you without a written agreement. If a dispute arises between you and the abandoned-property owner and you wind up in front of the judge, however, the case will be thrown out of court as soon as the judge discovers there is no written agreement.

Every state has a statute of frauds that says that for a real estate contract to be valid it must be in writing. If the real estate contract is not in writing, the real estate contract cannot be enforced in a court of law. If the contract cannot be enforced, the contract is not valid. If the contract is not valid, there is no contract. You get the picture.

Requirements of a Valid Contract

Besides the requirement that for a real estate contract to be valid it must be in writing, a valid real estate contract must meet four other requirements. We call this the CoCa CoLa test. We are not promoting or advertising a soft drink here but are using CoCa CoLa as a memory aid.

Once you understand these additional four requirements for a valid real estate contract, you will always use the CoCa CoLa test to make sure all the requirements are present in your real estate contracts. These requirements are *co*nsent, *ca*pacity, *co*nsideration, and *la*wful object.

CoCa CoLa

*Co*nsent: There must be mutual consent between the parties to the real estate contract. The parties to a real estate contract are typically the property owner and the buyer. The parties must agree (consent) to the wording and conditions written in the contract.

*Ca*pacity: The parties to the real estate contract must have the capacity to enter into the contract. This means the parties must be of sound mind (competent) and of legal age (18 in most places). There are some exceptions to the legal age requirement such as being married, or being married and then divorced, being in the military, or being an emancipated minor.

*Co*nsideration: Anything of value that influences a person to enter into a real estate contract is consideration. This could be money, a deed, a service, an item of personal property, an act (including the payment of money), or a promise (including the promise to pay on a loan). If the consideration is an act or a service, that act or service must be performed after the parties enter into the real estate contract.

Usually a buyer will attach some form of earnest money to the real estate contract to satisfy the consideration requirement.

This can be in the form of cash (we don't recommend cash), a check, a money order, or a promissory note.

We recommend the use of a promissory note for two reasons. First, by using a promissory note you protect your cash. Second, you don't have 10, 15, or 20 personal checks out there accompanying all those abandoned-property offers you are writing and presenting. You only have to turn the promissory note into cash if your offer is accepted and you are going to open an escrow.

> *La*wful: Real estate is lawful for people to buy and sell. For a real estate contract to be valid, the promises made between the parties must be legal to make. Also, the consideration given by the buyer must be legal to give. Now that you know the requirements of a valid contract, let's look into the various types of real estate contracts.

Types of Real Estate Contracts

There are many types of real estate contracts. The purpose of any real estate contract is to communicate. We believe that the simpler the real estate contract the better the communication between the parties to the contract. You could write a real estate contract on the back of a napkin sitting in a restaurant. We've done it. Unfortunately, the napkin got wet from moisture on the table and the ink blurred. Our contract was illegible. Better to use regular paper instead.

When we first got into the real estate business we used a four-page real estate purchase contract in California. We heard tell from the grizzled old real estate veterans that when they first got in the business, they used a one-page real estate purchase contract!

This contract was basically a blank piece of paper. You made up your offer as you wrote it. Talk about a simple real estate contract that would facilitate communication between the property owner and the buyer! What kind of a real estate contract should you use for your abandoned-property offers? We recommend you use a standard real estate purchase contract for your abandoned-property offers.

Real Estate Purchase Contract

A real estate purchase contract is the basic agreement between you and the property owner to purchase their property. Many variations of real estate purchase contracts exist. You can check with local Realtors, title insurance companies, or office supply stores to obtain a copy of the type of real estate purchase contract used in your area.

For example, in Texas, the Texas Real Estate Commission (TREC) provides a standard real estate purchase contract that must be used by all real estate licensees in Texas. However, the TREC real estate purchase contracts can be used by nonlicensees—real estate investors—to make offers. You can download TREC real estate contracts from their web site at www.trec.state.tx.us.

To obtain a standard-size contract format (8 1/2" × 11") see our book *How to Sell Your Home Without a Broker* (4th ed., John Wiley & Sons, 2004).

Remember, regardless of the type of real estate purchase contract you use, the purpose of the contract is to communicate. The more straightforwardly the real estate purchase contract states your intentions to the abandoned-property owner, the easier it will be for the property owner to understand what you are trying to do. If the property owner understands what you are trying to do with your offer, then it is more likely they will be predisposed to accept your offer. In other words, the simpler your real estate purchase contract the better.

Design

Real estate purchase contracts have been designed to have standard clauses known as the boilerplate, which are to be used for all types of transactions. The blank lines and spaces in the contract are to be used by you to customize your particular deal.

Whatever real estate purchase contract you are using, you begin to write by just filling in the blanks of the contract. Every blank space is either filled in, or the letters *NA* (not applicable) are written in. If you are using our contract, fill in city, state, and date. Then fill in the name of the buyer (that's you!).

And/Or Assigns

Now comes the exciting part! Before going any farther into the contract, we are going to stay in the "Received from" or buyer's section. We are going to add three words—*and/or assigns*—to this line. These are the three most powerful words you can have in a contract.

By adding *and/or assigns* to the buyer's name, we have created the opportunity for you to make money three ways rather than only one way. You can still make money the normal way by going ahead and buying the property yourself.

By adding *and/or assigns* you create a second way to make money. You can bring in a money partner to fund the transaction. You *and assigns*—the money partner—are now buying the property.

And/or assigns also gives you a third way to make money. You can assign the contract—you *or assigns*—for an assignment fee to another buyer. Now the other buyer is buying the property. You are not buying the property but assigning your interest in the purchase contract to another buyer and making money without buying or owning the property.

Assigning a contract is completely straightforward and legal. An assignment of a real estate purchase contract is designed to quickly provide a real estate solution for you and the abandoned-property owner. Remember our adage that the purpose of the contract is to communicate. When an abandoned-property owner asks you what *and/or assigns* means, this is what you should say:

And/Or Assigns Script

"_____ (abandoned-property owner's name), the AND/OR ASSIGNS clause gives both you and us the added flexibility of bringing in additional buyers or money partners to successfully close our transaction in a timely manner. Would that be all right with you?"

In our experience the abandoned-property owner's answer has always been yes. Sometimes we have had to work with an abandoned-property owner for a while and educate him or her on the benefits that *and/or assigns* had for them.

What do you do if the abandoned-property owner's answer is no? You want to make sure the abandoned-property owner understands what you are trying to do by having the ability to assign your contract. Flexibility is the name of the game in making a real estate deal work. This is especially true with an abandoned-property deal. If the abandoned-property owner will not agree to give you the flexibility you need by having *and/or assigns* in your contract, let the abandoned-property owner know that you will not proceed to present the rest of the contract.

You must stick to your guns on this point. (We're Texans.) *And/or assigns* is that important in your real estate investing success. It is much harder to come back to the negotiating table after you have already reached an agreement with the abandoned-property owner. Have *and/or assigns* be part of your contract from the beginning.

Real Estate Letter of Intent

A real estate letter of intent is our homage to the original one-page real estate purchase contract. Really, you can write anything you want in order to convey your intent to the abandoned-property owner that you are interested in purchasing their property.

We have found that writing a real estate letter of intent is the best way to approach an abandoned-property transaction. Today's real estate purchase contracts can be six, seven, eight or more pages in length. By using a real estate letter of intent you save time and effort. You typically find the abandoned property first; then you must track down the abandoned-property owner.

Write a real estate letter of intent after you find the property. Once you locate the abandoned-property owner, establish written contact with them using the real estate letter of intent. After you have received a positive response from the abandoned-property owner to your real estate letter of intent, then write a real estate purchase contract that spells out your complete offer.

A real estate letter of intent is not accompanied by consideration in the form of money. The real estate letter of intent is a precursor to a real estate option contract or a real estate purchase contract, both of which will be accompanied by some form of valuable consideration.

CoCa CoLa Test

If we apply the CoCa CoLa validity test to a real estate letter of intent, we will find a real estate letter of intent fails two tests. It fails the consent test because you are saying that you intend to buy the property but have no consent from the abandoned-property owner. It fails the consideration test because, as we have said, a real estate letter of intent is not accompanied by money. It is just a letter. So although a real estate letter of intent is not technically a valid contract, it meets our requirement that a real estate contract communicate between the parties.

We are going to give you several examples of a real estate letter of intent. We will start with the short and sweet. You can convey your intent in a very few words. We will then give an example of a real estate letter of intent with more words but still only two paragraphs in length.

And finally, we will give you an example of a real estate letter of intent that is three paragraphs in length and conveys lots of information. Your location and how much time you have will dictate the length of your real estate letter of intent.

Real Estate Letter of Intent 1

You decide you are interested in making an offer on the property. You want to put something in writing to protect yourself in the event another investor, a retail buyer, or even a real estate agent hoping to get a listing contract comes along before you have time to write and present an offer. This is what you (we) write:

To the Owners of 1511 Spring Avenue, Philadelphia, Pennsylvania.

We intend to make a cash offer on your property within the next 24 hours. In the event you receive another offer before we have had an opportunity to present our offer, we request you give us the first right of refusal and allow us to present our offer before you accept any other offer.

Sincerely,
Your name
Phone number
Today's date

Real Estate Letter of Intent 2

You may see other buyers looking at the abandoned property. Your goal is to have the abandoned-property owner focus on you and lose focus on other potential buyers. You want to intimidate the competition by writing your real estate letter of intent in their view. The other buyers will think you are writing an offer and may well bow out of the proceedings. Write this:

To the Owners of 1511 Spring Avenue, Philadelphia, Pennsylvania.

We intend to make a cash offer on your property within the next 24 hours. In the event you receive another offer before we have had an opportunity to present our offer, we request you give us the first right of refusal and allow us to present our offer before you accept any other offer.

Our offer will contain no contingencies regarding selling another property. We will close in 30 days or sooner. We will require a preliminary title report and clear title provided by you at the closing. We are real estate investors who have money partners and are already buying property in this area.

Sincerely,
Your name
Phone number
Today's date

Real Estate Letter of Intent 3

Real estate letter of intent 3 is designed to be written away from the property and is to be presented within 72 hours after you have visited the property. This letter is designed to inform the abandoned-property owner and to build in protections for you as the buyer.

Although paragraph two states that your offer is not contingent on your selling another property, paragraph three informs the abandoned-property owner that your offer will be contingent upon several important points. If these points cannot be resolved to your liking, you will not have to complete the deal. Write this:

> To the Owners of 1511 Spring Avenue, Philadelphia, Pennsylvania.
>
> We intend to make a cash offer on your property within the next 24 hours. In the event you receive another offer before we have had an opportunity to present our offer, we request you give us the first right of refusal and allow us to present our offer before you accept any other offer.
>
> Our offer will contain no contingencies regarding selling another property. We will close in 30 days or sooner. We will require a preliminary title report and clear title provided by you at the closing. We are real estate investors who have money partners and are already buying property in this area.
>
> Our offer will be contingent upon a structural pest-control inspection, a property inspection, and approval by our money partners. You will be responsible for removing all liens and encumbrances except current-year pro-rated property taxes.
>
> Sincerely,
> Your name
> Phone number
> Today's date

Real Estate Option Contract

A real estate option contract goes beyond a real estate letter of intent. More than conveying your intent to buy a property, a real estate option contract says you are buying property within a certain time frame. Also, you will commit funds in the form of an option fee or option money—basically a deposit—to keep the real estate option open.

Purpose

Our purpose here is to introduce you to the idea of using a real estate option contract as part of your real estate investing Brain Trust. See Chapter 16, "How to Option Abandoned Property," for a complete discussion about using lease options for your abandoned-property investments. Although a real estate option contract contains all the elements of CoCa CoLa to make it valid—consent, capacity, consideration, and lawful—it has a unique feature among all the different real estate contracts.

Unilateral Offer

A real estate option contract becomes a unilateral agreement once the optionor (abandoned-property owner) and optionee (you) sign the real estate option contract. All contracts are bilateral to begin with. Consent in the form of mutual agreement on both the abandoned-property owner's part and your part is necessary for validity.

Once the option has been agreed to, however, only you can exercise the option. The abandoned-property owner can't back out of the deal if you exercise the option.

The optionee (you) can back out of the deal and not be sued for specific performance. The optionor (the abandoned-property owner) gets to keep the option fee the optionee put up, but that's all.

Now it is time to turn our attention to presenting your abandoned-property offer—no matter in what format it exists—to the abandoned-property owner. In the next chapter, we will show you how to present your abandoned-property offer to ensure having it accepted by the abandoned-property owner.

CHAPTER 7

Presenting Your Abandoned-Property Offer

W e are going to give you a short course in real estate offer presentation. The purpose of presenting your abandoned-property offer is to have the abandoned-property owner accept your offer. By building rapport with the abandoned-property owner, you dramatically increase the likelihood that the abandoned-property owner will, eventually, accept your offer. This is referred to as a win-win tactic.

Building Rapport

You begin to build a rapport the moment you start an interaction with a person. We have found that smiling at, being respectful toward, and being interested in the abandoned-property owner's situation builds rapport. You also must be an encouraging and upbeat person when you interact with an abandoned-property owner to instill in the abandoned property-owner the confidence that you can get a real estate transaction done.

It may not be possible to build rapport face to face with the abandoned-property owner. After all, the abandoned-property owner has abandoned the property. However, we have found that the abandoned-property owner may still be local to the abandoned property.

We recommend that if the abandoned-property owner is local you meet with them in person. Although it is possible to build rapport over the phone, we have found that meeting with the abandoned-property owner in person is much more effective.

Presenting Your Abandoned-Property Offer

We are going to show you the where, when, and how of the abandoned-property offer presentation. What if the abandoned-property owner is not local to you or the abandoned property? Then you may have to present your abandoned-property offer over the phone, by fax, or by e-mail.

Keep the chitchat to no more than three minutes. At the appropriate time (see accompanying script) you will give the abandoned-property owner a copy of your offer so they can follow along with your presentation. You *are* going to make a presentation!

When to Present Your Offer

Present your abandoned-property offer within 72 hours of seeing the abandoned property for the first time. This is so you can convey a sense of urgency and interest to the abandoned-property owner.

It gets very easy to find abandoned property, look at the abandoned property, locate the abandoned-property owner, write your abandoned-property offer, get scared, and not present your offer to the abandoned-property owner.

Then you find another abandoned property, look at the abandoned property, locate the abandoned-property owner, write your abandoned-property offer, get scared . . .

Get the point? You will not make any money as an abandoned-property real estate investor unless you find abandoned property, look at the abandoned property, locate the abandoned-property owner, write your abandoned-property offer, *and* present your abandoned-property offer to the abandoned-property owner. Remember, *do it now, not later! Be bold!*

How to Present Your Offer

We want to give you a script to use when you present your abandoned-property offer to the abandoned-property owner. The script is the same no matter what kind of real estate contract you present.

Script

Pull out of your briefcase or folder two copies of your abandoned-property offer. Place them face down facing you on the table in front of you. Look at the abandoned-property owner and say:

"**Mr. and Mrs. Abandoned-Property Owner** [if you are on a first-name basis, use the abandoned-property owner's first name(s)]**, we are so excited to be able to present our offer to purchase your property today (tonight).**" Smile and pause for their response.

"**Thank you for allowing us to come into your home (or office).**" Smile and pause for their response.

"**As you know, we are real estate investors.**" Pause. "**Our offer is designed to solve your real estate problems.**" Pause. "**We want to do business with you.**" Pause and nod your head up and down.

Critical Portion
Now you are headed into the critical portion of your abandoned-property offer presentation. You are going to ask three questions of the abandoned-property owner. Your goal is to receive three "Yes" responses from the abandoned-property owner. If they answer "No" to any of your three questions and you cannot turn the no into a yes, there is no point in you presenting your abandoned-property offer.

Three Questions

1. "Before we go over our offer, we just want to make sure you still want to sell your property. Do you still want to sell your property?"

Pause and wait for the abandoned-property owner to answer "Yes."

If the abandoned-property owner says "No," your tendency will be to lose your composure and to ask them "**Why not?**" This question will only make the abandoned-property owner defensive and you will immediately lose the rapport between you.

If the abandoned-property owner says "No," ask this question: "**What happened?**" Listen very carefully to their response. Their answer will tell you if a deal can still be made.

Foreclosure Example

We found an abandoned property that was headed into foreclosure. From our interactions with the abandoned-property owner we thought they were ready to make a deal. When we got to this question, "Do you still want to sell your property?" they answered no.

We asked "What happened?" The abandoned-property owner answered that they wanted to try to save the property from foreclosure. Now we knew exactly what to do. We told the abandoned-property owner there were eight options to foreclosure.

We then asked their permission to present the eight foreclosure options. (If you get to this point and ask for permission to present further information and the abandoned-property owner will not give you their permission, don't give them the further information. You are wasting your time and their time.) They gave us their permission.

Eight Foreclosure Options

We told them the eight foreclosure options were reinstatement, redemption, deed in lieu of foreclosure, legal delay, bankruptcy, renegotiation, do nothing, or sell the property.

Part of your job as a real estate investor is to motivate the abandoned-property owner to take action that will benefit the property owner. Doing nothing is a form of action that in this situation has only negative results.

Your purpose with the foreclosure-options presentation is to have the abandoned-property owner conclude that selling you their property is their best and most profitable foreclosure option. This is better for the owner than losing their entire equity and damaging their credit at the same time.

After we presented the eight foreclosure options, the abandoned-property owner realized they had neither the money nor the time to do anything but sell us their property. We now had a yes answer to our first question "Do you still want to sell your property?" Now we could go on to question 2.

2. "Are you ready to go over our offer?"

Pause and wait for the abandoned-property owner to give you a second "Yes."

If the abandoned-property owner says "No," ask them this question: "**What happened?**" Listen very carefully to their response. Their answer will tell you if a deal can still be made.

Divorce Example
We were to the second question in our offer presentation with an abandoned-property owner, "Are you ready to go over our offer?" The abandoned-property owner answered no.

We asked "What happened?" The abandoned-property owner answered that he was getting a divorce. He became very emotional and started to cry. After a few minutes he composed himself. He then said he was ready to go over our offer. He had sole ownership of the property so could negotiate without the approval of his future ex.

If we had not stopped and listened to what was going on, we would have been presenting our offer to an abandoned-property owner who would have been too emotionally distraught to have heard what we were presenting. We then were able to go to question 3. (But first turn over the two copies of your abandoned-property offer which should be facing you and be upside down or sideways to the abandoned-property owner(s). Do not give them their copy yet!)

3. "If we can solve your real estate problems, can we do business?"

Pause and wait for the abandoned-property owner to give you a third "Yes".

If the abandoned-property owner says "No," ask them this question: "**What happened?**" Listen very carefully to their response. Again, their answer will tell you if a deal can still be made.

Expecting Another Offer Example
We were to the third question in our offer presentation with an abandoned-property owner, "If we can solve your real estate problems, can we do business?" The abandoned-property owner answered no.

We asked "What happened?" The abandoned-property owner answered that he was expecting another offer in the next few days and would take whichever offer was the best one. We now had a choice.

We could continue presenting our offer, or we could be insulted and leave without presenting our offer. We knew exactly what to do. We thanked the abandoned-property owner for their honesty.

We then asked them question 3 again. "If we can solve your real estate problems, can we do business?" This time they answered yes. We went on with our offer presentation. After receiving the third yes, give the abandoned-property owner their copy of your offer.

Your Offer

Now that you have laid the foundation by handling the where, the when, and the how of your abandoned-property offer, you can present the offer itself. We will reiterate that there is no point in you going over your abandoned-property offer if you have not received three yeses to the previous three critical questions.

Three Responses

There are three responses a property owner can have to your abandoned-property offer. The property owner can accept your offer, counter your offer, or reject your offer. If the property owner accepts your abandoned-property offer, you have a contract to take to a closing. If the property owner counters your abandoned-property offer, you have something to work with. If the property owner rejects your abandoned-property offer, you may be at a dead end. Obviously, you don't want the property owner to say no.

You cannot help the property owner solve their real estate problems without making money for yourself. You are a real estate investor not a real estate philanthropist. Don't buy the property owner's problems. The purpose of the script is to have the property owner be receptive to your offer. If the property owner does not accept your offer, talk over the sticking points and ask the property owner for a counteroffer.

Know what you and your money partners are prepared to do before you accept a counteroffer from the property owner. We have found that we can create a win-win for us and the property owner by using the script. Stick with the script!

In the next chapter, we will show you what to do when you are in a counteroffer situation. A counteroffer from the abandoned-property owner creates an opportunity for you to make a deal. Just because the property owner has accepted your abandoned-property offer or you have accepted the property owner's counteroffer does not mean you have made any money just yet.

CHAPTER 8

Counteroffers

In this chapter we will show you how to handle counteroffers. A counteroffer from the abandoned-property owner creates an opportunity for you to make an abandoned-property deal. We will also talk about your counteroffer to the abandoned-property owner's counteroffer. This is called the counter to the counter.

On the flip side of the coin, we will give you our take on how you should handle counteroffers. Once you either control or own an abandoned property and decide to assign your contract or option or flip or sell the property, you will receive offers.

Although it would be nice to think that every offer you receive is going to be exactly what you want, we all know that is not going to be the case. As part of your successful abandoned-property investing, you will make many counteroffers when you are on the seller side of the transaction.

We will also include in this chapter a conversation about backup offers. What do you do if the abandoned-property owner accepts a backup offer from another investor? This is very likely the case if the abandoned property in the deal is commercial, industrial, vacant land, or business property.

On the flip side of the coin with backup offers, we will give you our take on how you should handle backup offers you receive. Once you either control or own an abandoned property and decide to assign your contract or option or flip or sell the property, you will receive backup offers.

Counteroffers

Few abandoned-property owners receive exactly the terms they want or ask for when you make your first abandoned-property offer to them. If you understand from the beginning that you are likely to receive a counteroffer from the abandoned-property owner, you will probably find the process of counteroffering easier.

Even abandoned-property owners have expectations in such areas as price, terms, financing, inspections, contingencies, and closing date. For you to go into negotiations with the abandoned-property owner thinking that you are going to make only one offer on the property is a mistake. Your having a "they can take it or leave it attitude" will not create a win-win transaction.

Prepare for Counteroffers

When an abandoned-property owner makes a counteroffer to your abandoned-property offer, it indicates four points. The first and most obvious point is that the abandoned-property owner is not willing to accept your offer as written. The second point is that the abandoned-property owner is motivated to sell their abandoned property.

The third point is that the abandoned-property owner is willing to negotiate. Otherwise, they wouldn't have given you a counteroffer. The fourth point is that they desire different terms and conditions in the areas they have countered. It may be that they have accepted 80 percent, 90 percent, or more of your offer. They just have one or two sticking points to work out through the counteroffer.

1. Your Offer Is Unacceptable as Written

Anytime you present a real estate offer to an abandoned-property owner there are three responses you may receive.

The abandoned-property owner may accept your offer. They may reject your offer. They may counter your offer.

Receiving a counteroffer from the abandoned-property owner means they are not accepting your offer as written. However, it also means that they are not rejecting your offer.

Your Offer Is Rejected

Once an abandoned-property owner rejects your offer, you may be at a dead end for that deal. Your only alternative is to write another offer. You would then have to change the price and terms of your original offer.

However, then you will in essence be bidding against yourself. Many times we have made an offer on abandoned property that is not for sale. We have a value in mind before we make the offer.

Because there is no listed price, we have no idea what the abandoned-property owner thinks is a starting price for negotiation. That is why we are emphasizing the importance for you to have the abandoned-property owner give you a counteroffer.

2. The Abandoned-Property Owner Is a Motivated Seller

There is nothing more disheartening than being at a negotiating table and having the abandoned-property owner say "We reject your offer." We immediately know the abandoned-property owner is not motivated to make a deal.

When the abandoned-property owner gives you a counteroffer, you know they are motivated to make a deal. Perhaps they are not as motivated as you would like in that they didn't accept your offer outright with no changes. However, they are keeping the negotiations open by giving you their counteroffer.

3. The Abandoned-Property Owner Is Willing to Negotiate

We have said that the purpose of a real estate contract is to communicate. The purpose of a counteroffer also is to communicate. By giving you a counteroffer, the abandoned-property owner is keeping the lines of communication open.

A counteroffer is the physical written evidence that the abandoned-property owner is willing to negotiate. By meeting the written CoCa CoLa requirements, a counteroffer satisfies the test for contract validity. Now you know the abandoned-property owner is negotiating in good faith.

4. Your Offer May Be 80 Percent or More Accepted

The great news about a counteroffer is that the abandoned-property owner may be accepting 80 percent or more of your offer. Their counteroffer usually involves one, two, or three areas that they feel needs further negotiation.

Although receiving a counteroffer doesn't guarantee you have made an abandoned-property deal, you are well on your way to making that deal. Our experience with receiving a counteroffer from an abandoned-property owner is good; 80 percent of the time we receive a counteroffer from an abandoned-property owner when we put together a deal.

Understand Counteroffers

We keep on hand a two-page counteroffer that is designed to be combined with the offer. We recommend you always bring several blank counteroffers to your abandoned-property offer presentation.

Our goal is to walk out of every abandoned-offer presentation with a signed offer. In lieu of a signed offer, we want a signed counteroffer. By having blank counteroffers with us, we facilitate receiving a written counteroffer immediately.

What the Counteroffer Says

The counteroffer says the abandoned-property owner accepts all of the conditions and terms in our referenced offer with the following changes. The counteroffer is half blank. This is so the abandoned-property owner has room to write what changes to our offer they want to make.

The seller/abandoned-property owner retains the right to continue to offer the property for sale and accept other offers until we accept their counteroffer, and they in turn accept our acceptance. At the negotiating table we immediately sign the counteroffer from the seller if it meets our investment parameters. We now have made an abandoned-property deal.

Counter to the Counter

The counteroffer is where we sign agreeing to the counteroffer of the abandoned-property owner. It also gives us room to counter the counter. We put this in writing, and if they agree, they sign at the bottom of the document.

What the counteroffer form gives us is a way to finalize what we and the abandoned-property owner have negotiated. We recommend you stay at the negotiating table with the abandoned-property owner until you have completely worked out the deal. Then make sure you write it on the counteroffer.

Taking the Counteroffer with You

Sometimes all you can get at the offer presentation from the abandoned-property owner is a counteroffer, but the counteroffer may not be acceptable to you. You talk over the sticking points with the abandoned-property owner. You are hoping to write a counter to their counter. If you can't work it out, take the abandoned-property owner's written counteroffer with you.

Conditions Release

A conditions release is something we sometimes attach to our abandoned-property offers. We have found that in some abandoned-property offer situations we want to build in extra protections. These can include contingencies to our offer beyond those in a normal contract.

A conditions release gives the abandoned-property owner the opportunity to continue to offer their property for sale even after they have accepted our offer. If the abandoned-property owner receives another offer and accepts it, we will have 72 hours to remove any contingencies in our offer. Otherwise, we are out of the deal, and the abandoned-property owner can complete a sale with a new buyer.

Contingencies

We sometimes add one or more contingencies to our abandoned-property offer. These include that our offer is subject to the approval of our money partners, attorney, or CPA.

We put a contingency or contingencies into our offer when we are unsure of what we may be getting into. That way, if we have bitten off more than we can chew, we have a way to extricate ourselves from a bad deal.

Contingencies Example

We put together an offer on a commercial piece of property that had been abandoned in Fort Worth, Texas, after a tornado had caused damage. We thought we knew what we were getting into going into the deal. Because of the size of the deal, we put in our three contingencies.

Our offer was subject to the approval of our money partners, attorney, and CPA. We were told by the abandoned-property owner that there might be a potential asbestos problem with the property and they were also taking backup offers.

Our CPA signed off on the deal. Our attorney signed off on the deal. Our money partners would not sign off on the deal. They had been involved in a previous investment that entailed asbestos cleanup. The final cost had tripled the initial estimates. They had lost money on that deal.

We reluctantly informed the abandoned-property owner that we were not going to go through with the deal because our money partners would not sign off. The property was sold to another group. We were very disappointed.

When the other group got into the building, the asbestos problem mushroomed. Not only was there asbestos in the ceilings, there was asbestos in the walls and floors. There was asbestos in the heating and air-conditioning systems. There was asbestos in the ductwork. The EPA got involved. We thanked our lucky stars that our contingencies had gotten us off the hook.

Counteroffer Logistics

There are six areas to understand about counteroffer logistics that will help you handle counteroffers more effectively. These six areas are changes or amendments, writing a counteroffer, revoking a counteroffer, accepting another purchase offer, buyers accepting counteroffers, and timing.

1. Changes or Amendments

If the counteroffer changes or amendments to an offer are relatively simple and relatively few, use a simple form. If the changes or amendments are extensive, then we recommend you rewrite a new offer incorporating the changes.

Order

1. List the sections and changes on the counteroffer in the order in which they appear in the real estate contract. By doing this, the counteroffer may be more easily understood. Legally, changes and amendments may be made in any order.
2. Write the section number and letter designation as well as the section caption. Designations and captions are most easily understood if listed in the same order as those in the real estate purchase contract you want

to change. This also makes the sections of the offer easier to locate. Technically, the numbers and letters are not intended to be part of the contract.

3. Write the changes and amendments you want to make for the section you listed. Be definite and specific.

2. Writing a Counteroffer

When making or receiving a counteroffer, be aware of these points. The counteroffer must be in writing. Like offers, counteroffers are not valid unless written. The length of time buyers have to accept the counteroffer should be stated clearly. Sellers usually offer an acceptance time ranging from several hours to several days.

3. Revoking a Counteroffer

A seller may revoke their counteroffer any time before buyers accept their counteroffer *and* communicate their acceptance of the seller's counteroffer in writing.

4. Accepting Another Purchase Offer

A seller may accept another offer as long as buyers to whom the seller made a counteroffer have not accepted the counteroffer. Until the seller receives a copy of this counteroffer accepted and signed by the buyers, the seller has the right to continue to market the property described in the purchase offer for sale. The seller can accept any offer that is acceptable to them.

5. Buyers Accepting Counteroffers

To establish a binding legal contract, the buyers must accept and communicate their acceptance to the seller in writing. They must do this within the time limits allowed by the seller's counteroffer and before the seller revokes the counteroffer.

6. Timing

The seller and the buyer may continue to make as many counteroffers as they want. This can be done until an agreement on
the terms is reached or a decision to discontinue the process
is made.

To summarize:

1. Make or accept only *written* offers or counteroffers.
2. State clearly the length of time a buyer has to accept
   the seller's counteroffer.
3. Choose the form to use depending on the changes
   involved. Use a counteroffer form to make counteroffers for which the changes are relatively few and simple. Write a counteroffer using a real estate purchase
   contract for changes that are numerous or complex.
4. Sellers may revoke their counteroffer any time within
   the time limits specified in the contract before buyers accept the seller's counteroffer *and* communicate
   their acceptance.
5. Buyers may also revoke their offer any time within
   the time limits specified in the contract before the
   seller accepts their offer *and* communicates their
   acceptance.

Backup Offers

Backup offers are offers that sellers accept in a secondary position to the offer they accepted previously. Sellers may want to
accept backup offers because of the possibility that a contract
may become void in some way.

Voiding

Voiding can occur because contingencies in the primary
purchase agreement are not satisfied or some other com-
plication occurs. When the first offer fails, the next offer in
line automatically becomes the primary offer.

In our offer on the commercial property that had been abandoned in Fort Worth, the abandoned-property owner accepted a backup offer two days after they accepted our offer. They gave us 72 hours to remove our three contingencies. Remember, our offer was subject to the approval of our money partners, attorney, and CPA.

When our money partners said no to the deal, we were out. Our offer was off the table. The backup offer the abandoned-property owner had accepted became the primary offer. This saved us from getting any heat from the abandoned-property owner.

Taking Backup Offers

If you decide you want to accept backup offers, consider doing the following:

1. Tell the buyers from whom you accept the primary offer that you plan to accept backup offers.
2. Negotiate backup offers in the same way you negotiated the primary purchase offer.
3. Include a clause noting that it is a backup offer and, as such, is subject to the nonperformance of any previous offers.
4. Include a statement allowing buyers to withdraw a backup offer in writing at any time before you notify them that their offer is in first position.
5. Number each backup offer as you accept it to avoid priority disputes.
6. Tell all the other offerers, including the actual buyers, when you accept another backup offer.

In the next chapter, we will show you how to negotiate with the abandoned-property owner in foreclosure. We have found that 9 out of 10 abandoned-property owners are in foreclosure or are going into foreclosure. There may be an opportunity to buy their property or buy their equity in the property before the foreclosure sale takes place.

CHAPTER 9

Negotiating with the Abandoned-Property Owner in Foreclosure

In this chapter we will teach you how to negotiate with abandoned-property owners in foreclosure. We have found that 9 out of 10 abandoned-property owners are in foreclosure or are going into foreclosure. There may be an opportunity to buy their property or buy their equity in the property before the foreclosure sale takes place.

Once you have contacted an abandoned-property owner who is in the preforeclosure phase either by phone, letter, or in person and set up an appointment, your next step is to prepare for a face-to-face negotiating meeting. This meeting is for you to develop rapport, demonstrate expertise, and set the stage for putting a win-win offer together.

After we show you how to prepare for the meeting, we will show you how to make the foreclosure-options presentation. Negotiating with the abandoned-property owner then becomes a simple task of helping them chose their best option. Of course, the best option for you is to have the abandoned-property owner agree to sell their property or their equity to you. It is important to realize, however, that you may not wind up making a deal right away.

Benefits to the Abandoned-Property Owner

Many of the foreclosure options benefit only the abandoned-property owner. We have found that even when we help an abandoned-property owner and don't come away with a deal for us, we still benefit. Sometimes, the abandoned-property owner solves their foreclosure problem only temporarily. If they can't resolve the root cause of the problem that led to the foreclosure to begin with, they are likely to wind up in foreclosure again. In our experience, this occurs 90 percent of the time.

Whom do you think they will call the next time they are in trouble? They will call us (you). We helped them the first time. Maybe we can help them the second time. If there is nothing they can do to avoid an impending foreclosure sale, who do you think has the inside track on making a good real estate investment?

Preparation for the Meeting

Obtain all necessary information. This should include a copy of the notice of default (if any), a property profile from a title insurance company, and confirmation of property taxes paid or owed. Bring any pictures of the property that you have taken. Bring the comparable sales information you have compiled from a real estate agent or title company.

Include any letters of testimonial you have received from prior transactions. If you also have character letters, bring them, too. Itemize the costs to repair and improve the property to salable condition. Estimate the costs for holding, marketing, and selling the property. Always include real estate commissions, which can be substantial.

Put together a presentation book, which includes all of these items. Add to it the foreclosure-options presentation and questions for the abandoned-property owner. Although you may not use or need all the information at the meeting, we have found it is much better to be overprepared than underprepared.

Questions for the Abandoned-Property Owner

We recommend you ask and get the answers to the following five questions at the beginning of the meeting. The answers may help you to determine if you should continue with the meeting or what direction to emphasize during the meeting.

1. *"Are you aware of the impending foreclosure?"*

You would be surprised at some of the answers we have received to this question. Some people stick their head in the sand and want to pretend that everything is going to be all right.

We had one abandoned-property owner tell us that they mailed the keys to their house to the lender with a note that they couldn't afford the payments and were abandoning the property. They honestly believed that would take care of everything!

Most people do not know the timeline for the foreclosure process. Some people think they have all the time in the world. We are there to assure them that time is really of the essence for their situation.

2. *"Do you know what you will have to do to protect your interests?"*

Most people do not have a clue about what they can do to protect their interests in their property. This question introduces the foreclosure-options presentation.

Some people have a completely mistaken idea of what they can do. Other people are resigned to the fact that there is nothing they can do, even when that isn't true. After all, they have abandoned the property.

3. *"Are you willing to take the time and effort to fight the foreclosure?"*

When people are facing foreclosure, there may be many other pressing problems occurring at the same time. There may be a job loss or an illness in the family. Just having enough money to buy food and keep the lights on may be a struggle. Having the time, energy, and resources to fight a foreclosure action may just not be possible for them.

4. "If we were able to get you cash, would you be willing to sell your equity to us at a discount?"

This is a testing question. You want the abandoned-property owner to come to grips with the fact that they may have to make a deal. You are also letting them know that you are there as a real estate investor who must make a profit to be able to help them.

5. "If you feel comfortable working with us, is there any reason you can see why we couldn't do business?"

This is a trial closing question. You want the abandoned-property owner to say that if they feel comfortable with you there is no reason they can see why you couldn't do business. However, the question will also elicit other useful information.

You may discover that the owner is going to deed the property to his brother-in-law for a quick $5,000. They are meeting with you because they want to hear about their foreclosure options besides the brother-in-law route.

They may also say that they have an agreement with another investor and want to see if you are going to make them a better offer. Now you know who your competition is.

At the Meeting

Once we have asked the owner the five questions and received their answers, we proceed to the foreclosure-options presentation, if it is appropriate. We have decided on several occasions to cut short the meeting without making the foreclosure-options presentation.

The abandoned-property owner may tell us they will not sell their equity to us at a discount. They may say they already have a deal. They may tell us that they will not do business with us even if they feel comfortable. We may feel we are wasting our time. The point is you will have to decide whether to stay or go.

Foreclosure Options

There are eight actions the abandoned-property owner may take in response to a notice of default. We use the foreclosure-options presentation once we are in front of the abandoned-property owner. We recommend that you put each of these eight options on a separate sheet of paper.

1. Reinstatement

The reinstatement option gives the abandoned-property owner the opportunity to make up back payments plus any incidental charges, such a filing or posting notices and trustee service charges. The payment of the reinstatement amount will cancel the foreclosure and enable the borrower to continue as if no default occurred.

2. Redemption

To redeem the loan, the borrower must pay off the loan in full. This may be accomplished through refinancing (with a cosigner perhaps) or by a relative or friend bailing out the owner in return for an equity position. Most states permit redemption up to the foreclosure sale.

3. Deed in Lieu of Foreclosure

For the abandoned-property owner who knows they will have no opportunity to reinstate, redeem, or even sell their property and just wants out of the property, a deed in lieu of foreclosure may be a viable foreclosure alternative. Sometimes the abandoned-property owner can turn the ownership of the property over to the bank and avoid the trauma of foreclosure.

4. Legal Delay

If the abandoned-property owner can prove that the amount in default is inaccurate, they can delay the foreclosure proceeding and gain additional time to find a more acceptable solution. The maximum time extension is effectively the time it would take to start the foreclosure process over again.

5. File Bankruptcy

Although this is not a permanent cure, filing bankruptcy can temporarily halt the foreclosure process. Before considering this option, the abandoned-property owner should seek the advice of an attorney.

Foreclosure Stops
The moment an abandoned-property owner in default files a petition for bankruptcy, foreclosure proceedings stop immediately. This results from a legal moratorium called an automatic stay imposed by the bankruptcy court. It prevents creditors from pursuing any legal actions to enforce their claims against a debtor.

6. Renegotiate with the Lender

The most overlooked of all the foreclosure options an abandoned-property owner has is the opportunity to renegotiate with their lender. The lender does not want the property back, and any effort by the abandoned-property owner to negotiate a plan that will enable the loan to be back in service for the lender's loan portfolio will be looked upon with great favor by the lender.

7. Do Nothing

The abandoned-property owner always has the choice of just letting things happen. They will surely lose their hard-earned equity and damage their credit. They can just about forget getting a new home anytime in the foreseeable future.

Unfortunately, we have encountered more than a few people who just bury their heads in the sand. They think they are going to win the lottery. They procrastinate until there are no viable options left to prevent the foreclosure sale.

Part of your job as a real estate investor is to motivate the abandoned-property owner to take action that will benefit the abandoned-property owner. Doing nothing is a form of action that in this situation has only negative results.

8. Sell the Property

For the abandoned-property owner who doesn't care to save their property or who has no other choice but to let the property go, selling the property may be the smartest choice. This is true even if they have to sell the property at a bargain price.

Your purpose with the foreclosure-options presentation is to have the abandoned-property owner come to the conclusion that selling you their property is their best and most profitable foreclosure option.

After you have made the foreclosure-options presentation, now is the time to ask the abandoned-property owner some additional questions. Your intention is really to help them make a decision.

Because time is of the essence for the abandoned-property owner, having them make a decision is in their best interest. You are doing them a disservice if you allow them to sell you the "they want to think about it" line.

It has been our experience that when people say they want to think about it, they never do. We have nothing against people thinking. People use "think about it" as a way of procrastinating. There is no room to procrastinate in the foreclosure arena, especially when you are the person facing foreclosure!

Additional Questions

We ask the abandoned-property owner three additional questions:

1. Which of the foreclosure options do you think makes the most sense for your situation?

If they answer with option eight—sell the property—we offer to buy their property. If they answer with anything other than option eight, we ask the next question.

2. Do you have the time and financial resources to carry out the foreclosure option you think makes the most sense?

If they cannot answer yes to both the time portion and the financial-resources portion of the question, we tell them that the foreclosure option is not going to work. We then offer to buy their property. If they answer yes to both the time and financial resources portions of the question, we ask them the next question.

3. Do they want our help in carrying out the foreclosure option they have decided on?

You have to be careful here. You cannot give the abandoned-property owner legal advice unless you are an attorney. You don't want to get too involved because you open yourself to liability if things don't work out well for the abandoned-property owner. Plus, you can't waste your time helping them without making any money.

When the abandoned-property owner says yes, they want our help, we have found that what works best for us is to give them the names of several attorneys that specialize in helping people in foreclosure. We leave the abandoned-property owner our contact information and keep open the possibility that we will buy their property.

When the abandoned-property owner says no, they do not want our help, we have found that what works best for us is leaving them our contact information and keeping open the possibility that we will buy their property. In other words, we are flexible, knowing the abandoned-property owner may indeed call us back and offer to sell us their property.

The Abandoned-Property Owner Wants to Sell Their Property

We have an abandoned-property owner who is in the foreclosure process and wants to sell us their property. What do we want to buy? Do we want to buy their property? Or do we want to buy their equity? Our first choice is we want to buy their equity.

Why don't we want to buy their property? It is not that we are uninterested in buying the property. We will buy the property as our second choice. We are primarily interested in making quick cash. The property includes too many liabilities, such as a loan that is in the foreclosure process.

What Is the Abandoned-Property Owner's Equity?

The abandoned-property owner's equity is the difference between the value of their property and any monetary liens or encumbrances against their title to the property. If an abandoned-property owner owns a property free and clear, their equity equals the value of the property.

Because the abandoned-property owner we are dealing with is in foreclosure, there is a monetary lien in the form of a mortgage or trust deed against their title to the property. Their equity is the value of the property minus the mortgage balance minus the back payments minus any foreclosure expenses that have already accumulated.

In a nonforeclosure situation, if the retail value of the property is $350,000 and the mortgage balance against the property is $240,000, the owner's equity is $110,000.

Nonforeclosure Situation

Retail Value	$350,000
Mortgage	−$240,000
Owner's Equity	$110,000

In a foreclosure situation, the value of a property is no longer the retail value. The property may be run-down. The abandoned-property owner does not have the luxury of a normal marketing time to bring in the highest price. In other words, the value of the property is lowered automatically in a foreclosure situation. Let's say the value of the property is now $320,000 to $325,000.

The mortgage lien goes up in a foreclosure situation. The missed payments are added to the remaining balance of the mortgage. If the missed payments total $20,000, then the mortgage lien is now $260,000.

If the lender has formally initiated the foreclosure process, there are foreclosure expenses added to the mortgage balance. Let's say these foreclosure expenses are $4,000. Now the total mortgage balance is $264,000. Now the abandoned-property owner's equity is substantially reduced.

Foreclosure Situation

Foreclosure Value	$320,000
Mortgage	−$264,000
Abandoned-Property Owner's Equity	$56,000

Instead of the equity being $110,000 in the nonforeclosure situation, the equity is $56,000 in the foreclosure situation. The abandoned-property owner has suffered a $54,000 loss in equity.

Equity Loss

Nonforeclosure Equity	$110,000
Foreclosure Equity	−$56,000
Equity Loss	$54,000

Please be clear on what we are saying here. The abandoned-property owner has suffered the equity loss. With a new owner back in control of the property, who is not in a foreclosure situation, the value of the property goes back up. When the value of the property goes back up, the owner's equity increases dollar for dollar.

Your Offer

You are going to offer the abandoned-property owner $18,000 for their $56,000 equity. If you keep the property, you are going to have to pay the lender the $24,000 in back payments and foreclosure expenses to stop the foreclosure. Now you will have $42,000 in the property. If you must make repairs and do fix-up, you may have $3,000 to $5,000 more involved.

Then you add in mortgage payments, property-tax payments, and insurance payments. Resale costs could add another $20,000 to $25,000 or more to your investment. When you add this all up, your total is $67,000!

Your Offer

Cash to Owner	$18,000
Cash to Lender	$24,000
Repairs and Fix-Up Costs	$5,000
Carrying and Resale Costs	+$20,000
Total Invested	$67,000

This becomes a negotiating tool for you with the abandoned-property owner. Your point is that the maximum you can offer them is $18,000 cash for their equity. By giving them $18,000 for their equity, you will have $67,000 in the property before you make any money!

We have found that when we show the abandoned-property owner these types of figures, they are much more amenable to accepting our offer. We are not trying to be mean to them or take advantage of them. We are trying to help them. But we (you) can't help them if we (you) can't make any money. Otherwise, we (you) will be in a foreclosure situation ourselves!

Making Money

Speaking of making money, let's look at the numbers. The mortgage balance is back to $240,000 (actually a little lower because the back payments reduced the principal, but really not worth mentioning).The property restored to retail value is now worth $350,000 (or perhaps a bit more).

Retail Buyer

If we sell the property to a retail buyer, we will make a $1100,000 gross profit minus the $67,000 invested, which equals a $43,000 net profit.That is a 64 percent return perhaps over a three-month to six-month time period.That makes the investment worth the risk.

Making Money with a Retail Buyer

Sales Price	$350,000
Mortgage	−$240,000
Gross Profit	$110,000
Money Invested	−$67,000
Net Profit	$43,000

Assign Contract to Wholesale Buyer

If we assign the contract to a real estate investor who rehabs property, we will have paid no cash to the abandoned-property owner, no cash to the lender, no repairs and fix-up costs, and no carrying and resale costs. Do you think it is possible to flip our contract for $5,000 to $10,000? We did exactly that.

Making Money with a Wholesale Buyer

Assignment Fee	$10,000
Mortgage	−0
Gross Profit	$10,000
Money Invested	−0
Net Profit	$10,000

In the next chapter, we will show you how to buy the abandoned property first then get a buyer. This is a corollary to our real estate investment axiom *Buy the property first, then get the financing.* In other words, have the abandoned-property owner sign your contract then worry about getting a buyer.

CHAPTER 10

Buy the Abandoned Property First, Then Get a Buyer

We are going to introduce you to our real estate investment axiom: *Buy the property first, then get the financing.* The abandoned-property corollary to this axiom is *buy the abandoned property first, then get a buyer.*

When you follow these axioms it makes it easier to write offers. You don't have to fear what you are going to do if your offer is accepted! Writing an offer is the way to tie up a property. When you tie up a property you control a property.

Buy the Abandoned Property First, Then Get a Buyer

Example 1

We found a four-bedroom, two-and-one-half-bathroom, single-family home. The property was abandoned and headed to foreclosure. The retail value of the property was $223,000. The abandoned-property owner had an assumable Veterans Administration (VA) loan with a remaining balance of $167,000. They were $5,000 behind in their payments. They owed a total of $172,000 on their mortgage. Their equity position was $51,000.

Owner's Equity Position

Retail Value	$223,000
First Mortgage	−$172,000
Owner's Equity Position	$51,000

When we called on the real estate sign and the agent asked us what we were prequalified for, this was our response (and will be yours). We told the agent that we were real estate investors. If the property met our parameters, we had the financial resources, along with our money partners, to buy the property.

We set up an appointment with the agent and the abandoned-property owner. We made the foreclosure-options presentation. At the end of our presentation, the abandoned-property owner said they would like to sell us their property.

Our Offer

We offered them no money down and agreed to take over payments on the loan and make up the $5,000 in back payments. They accepted our offer. They agreed to pay their agent the real estate commission.

We did not have to qualify for a new loan. We did not have to qualify to take over the existing VA loan. We did not have to come up with a down payment. We made an offer that worked for us.

We let the abandoned-property owner decide whether to accept our offer. We and you may not have accepted our offer. Why they accepted our offer was their business.

Then Get a Buyer

We now had a property available to flip. Only by making an offer can you start the process of flipping a property. We flipped the property for $205,000 within two weeks to a retail buyer who was going to live in the property.

The buyer was going to assume the VA loan on the property. The buyer was actually a veteran. They were going to use their VA eligibility to assume the loan. The buyer was very happy to get a good deal. The abandoned-property owner was happy because they were out from under the foreclosure with no deficiency judgment hanging over their heads. We were happy because we had made $23,000.

Our Profit

Sales Price	$195,000
Purchase Price	$167,000
Back Payments	−$5,000
Our Profit	$23,000

Example 2

We found a three-bedroom, two-bathroom condominium. The property was in foreclosure. The lender had sent the first formal notice-of-default letter. The owners were in a panic. They were thinking of abandoning the property.

The retail value of the property was $425,000. The first mortgage on the property had a remaining balance of $345,000. The owners were $19,000 behind in their payments. Their equity position was $61,000.

Owner's Equity Position

Retail Value	$425,000
First Mortgage	$345,000
Back Payments	−$19,000
Owner's Equity Position	$61,000

Our Offer

We offered the owners $11,000 for their equity in the form of a promissory note secured by a second trust deed on the property. The promissory note was a straight note for five years. This means there were no payments until the final balloon payment of principal and interest at the end of the five years.

We also agreed to pay the $19,000 in back payments and reinstate the loan. The total cash out of our pocket was $19,000. Remember the $11,000 we offered the owners for their equity was a promissory note and not cash. We were not worried about this promissory note because we were going to flip the property.

Then Get a Buyer

We flipped the property for $405,000. The buyer was a real estate investor who was planning to rent the property. They assumed the first mortgage of $345,000 from the lender and our second mortgage of $11,000 to the owners.

We were now off the hook to pay the owners. Because the $11,000 second mortgage had no payments, the real estate investor would be able to have a positive cash flow.

How did we make out on this deal? We invested $19,000 cash and received our money back plus a $30,000 profit. The owners avoided foreclosure and had $11,000 plus interest coming his way five years down the road. The investor was happy because they got a good deal.

Our Profit

Sales Price	$405,000
First Mortgage	$345,000
Second Mortgage	$11,000
Back Payments	−$19,000
Our Profit	$30,000

Some of you are thinking, "why didn't you guys hold onto the property like the investor you flipped the property to, rent it out, and have a positive cash flow?" That is good thinking if you are using the long-term wealth-building strategy. We had a quick-cash strategy at the time, so landlording was not on our agenda.

Example 3

Early on in our real estate investing career, we tied up a five-bedroom, four-bathroom, single-family home with a pool. The owners were in preforeclosure. We negotiated a deal with the owners and bought their equity. We then spent $14,000 fixing up the property.

We are presenting this example as our coaching you on what not to do. This was not one of our finest hours. We were still in the more traditional mindset of trying to make everyone in the deal happy. By the time this deal blew up, no one was happy.

Then Get a Buyer

We found retail buyers who said they were in love with the house. To make the deal work, we agreed to repaint the inside and outside of the house—which we had just repainted—the colors the buyers wanted.

We also agreed to run a natural-gas line to the utility room so the buyer could use their gas dryer. Finally, we had a tree removed from the pool area because the buyers were concerned that the roots were going to crack the bottom of the pool.

Can you guess what happened? The buyers came down with a disease all retail buyers get during the course of a real estate transaction. Some buyers get a mild case of the disease. Some buyers get a severe case of the disease. Unfortunately for us, these particular buyers came down with a terminal case of the disease.

Buyer's Remorse

What is this dreaded disease? Buyer's remorse! Every buyer experiences the onset of the disease once their offer is accepted by the seller. Even as a real estate investor, you will experience buyer's remorse. There is no known antidote or medication. The disease just has to run its course.

The symptoms of buyer's remorse usually strike at night, when a buyer is about to go to sleep. Sometimes the symptoms strike after the buyer has fallen asleep and they awaken as if from a nightmare.

The buyers start having doubts about the purchase. Are they doing the right thing? Should they look at more properties? Did they offer too much? Can they really afford the monthly payments? Is the house big enough? Is the house too big?

They start to sweat. They get out of bed and get a drink of water. They go back to bed, but they can't fall asleep. The questions begin swirling again in their heads. What if they don't qualify for a loan? What if they *do* qualify for a loan? Who is going to take care of the pool? What if the pool does leak?

In our case, three weeks after we had accepted the buyers' offer and three days after we had finished repainting, installing the gas line, and removing the tree, the buyers backed out. Their case of remorse became terminal for them and for us. Our deal was dead.

Bottom line: Provide allowances for the work to be done *after* closing, if you must, to make the deal work, but don't spend your time or money on it before closing. Oh yes, and our profit on this deal? Don't ask. You got the point, right?

Wholesale Buyers

We actually prefer flipping our abandoned properties to wholesale buyers. Wholesale buyers do not get buyer's remorse. (Well maybe a little bit.) We know some of you are thinking, "Wait a minute. How can you make any money flipping real estate to wholesale buyers? Don't wholesale buyers want to pay a wholesale price."

We do flip our abandoned-property deals at a wholesale price to wholesale buyers! We are not greedy about it. We prefer to do many smaller deals and make a quick profit rather than one or two big deals that are time-consuming and entail more risk.

We have come to appreciate that being successful real estate investors is strictly a numbers game. Although we prefer to flip our abandoned-property deals to other investors for all the reasons we just talked about, we are still smart people.

Our marketplace is retail and wholesale buyers. The more buyers you have in your potential pool, the more likely you will be able to flip your abandoned-property deals successfully.

Negotiating with the Owner's Lender

Next we are going to show you how to negotiate with the abandoned-property owner's lender before the foreclosure sale. This may be before or after you have put together an agreement with the abandoned-property owner to buy their equity or their property.

Negotiating Before You Put the Agreement Together

We suggest negotiating with the lender before you have put any agreement together with the abandoned-property owner. That way you know how the lender is going to behave. This will eliminate any nasty surprises from the lender down the road. You will need the abandoned-property owner's permission to speak with their lender.

Although we recommend that you dispose of properties quickly, especially foreclosures, you may have to hold on to a property longer than you planned. One of the most important areas to negotiate is how the lender is going to respond if you buy the abandoned-property owner's equity and want to take over the existing loan. Most real estate loans have a due-on-sale clause and/or a prepayment penalty.

If the lender wants to play hardball, they can begin foreclosure proceedings against you if you don't agree with what they want to do with the loan vis-à-vis interest rates, assumption fees, payment amounts, or prepayment penalties. We are going to give you an overview of the due-on-sale clause. We will also show you the difference between an assumable loan and a subject-to loan. And what is a prepayment penalty, anyway?

Due-on-Sale Clause

A due-on-sale clause is a type of acceleration clause in a promissory note, mortgage note, trust deed, or mortgage contract that gives a lender the right to demand all sums owed to be paid immediately if the owner transfers title to the property.

The legality of the due-on-sale clause was argued all the way to the U.S. Supreme Court in the 1980s. To unify all the states under one legal interpretation, Congress passed the Garn-St. Germain lending bill in 1986. Unfortunately, the due-on-sale clause is legal. It can be enforced by the lenders.

Assumable Loan

An assumable loan is an existing promissory note or mortgage note secured by a trust deed or mortgage contract, respectively, that is kept at the same interest rate and terms as when the original borrower financed the property.

When you assume a loan, you become primarily liable for the payments and any deficiency judgment arising from a loan default. The borrower/owner becomes secondarily liable for the payments and any deficiency judgment.

Remember, a deficiency judgment is a court decision making an individual personally liable for the payoff of a remaining amount due because less than the full amount was obtained by foreclosure on the property.

Lenders typically charge an assumption fee for you to assume a loan. They also want you to qualify for the loan, as if you were originating a new loan rather than assuming an existing loan.

Subject-to Loan

A subject-to loan is an existing loan for which the buyer agrees to take over responsibility for payments under the same terms and conditions as existed when the original borrower financed the property. However, the original borrower remains primarily responsible for any deficiency judgment in the event of a loan default.

The name *subject-to loan* comes from the fact that the buyer takes over the existing loan subject-to the same terms and conditions. The interest rate is the same. The monthly payments are the same. Everything about the loan stays the same. There is no lender approval required for you to take over a loan subject-to as there is when you assume a loan.

We say it this way: When you assume a loan, you are entering into a formal agreement with the lender. When you take over a loan subject-to, there is no formal agreement with the lender. Subject-to loans do not have a due-on-sale clause in their paperwork.

Therefore, the lender cannot threaten you with calling the loan "due on sale" when you have made a deal with the owner to transfer title. Pre-1988 VA guaranteed loans and pre-1986 Federal Housing Administration (FHA) insured loans are subject-to loans. Also, many privately held owner-financing loans may be subject-to loans.

Prepayment Penalty

A prepayment penalty is a fine imposed on a borrower by a lender for early payoff of a loan or any early payoff of a substantial part of the loan. To find out if there is a prepayment penalty on a loan, as with the due-on-sale clause, check the loan documents. Most prepayment penalties lapse once the loan is on the books for five years.

The amount of the prepayment penalty is usually stated as a certain number of months' interest in addition to the amount remaining on the loan as of the payoff date. Prepayment penalties can be six months' interest or more. This can be quite a substantial amount.

What is the prepayment penalty on a loan if the remaining loan balance is $200,000, the annual interest rate is 7 percent, and the prepayment penalty is six months' interest?

Prepayment Penalty

Loan Balance	$200,000
Interest Rate	×7%
Annual Interest	$14,000
Six Months' Interest	$7,000

A lender cannot legally enforce receiving a prepayment penalty as a result of a foreclosure sale. The problem for you as a real estate investor is that the prohibition on the lender receiving a prepayment penalty as a result of a foreclosure sale is lifted if you buy the owner's equity in preforeclosure.

Whipsaw Effect

A lender can have an owner/borrower—or in this case, you, an investor—caught between the due-on-sale clause and the prepayment penalty. As you attempt to help the owner out of a foreclosure situation, we have suggested you buy their equity. You may encounter what we call the whipsaw effect with the lender.

If you try to take over the owner's existing loan subject-to and it is not a subject-to loan, the lender can call the loan all due and payable using the due-on-sale clause. If you tell the lender you are going to pay off the loan, and the loan is less than five years old and stipulates a prepayment penalty, you may get stuck paying the prepayment penalty!

Negotiating after You Put the Agreement Together

You may prefer negotiating with the lender after you have put together an agreement with the owner. Some investors find it a waste of time to negotiate with the lender before they have put together an agreement with the owner. After they have their ducks lined up with the lender, they have found when they go back to the owner they cannot reach an agreement to buy the owner's equity.

Talking to the Lender

The earlier in the foreclosure process the lender is contacted, the better it is for the borrower. Sometimes a borrower will call their lender and say, "We haven't missed a payment yet, but we are afraid we are about to." Lenders agree that they want to know about a borrower's financial distress well ahead of the borrower missing that first loan payment.

As far as the lender is concerned, this is the perfect time for the owner in distress to call them. A spokeswoman for Fannie Mae puts it this way: "Don't hide from your lender. If you contact your loan servicer, most of the time you will stay in your home."

After you receive an owner's permission to talk to their lender, we suggest the following approach. Call them up and identify yourself as a real estate investor who is working with the owner. Find out from the lender exactly where the owner is in the foreclosure process.

It has been our experience that half the time some type of loan work-out plan is put together between the lender and the owner. The other half of the time when a loan work-out plan is not put together is when you have your opportunity to make money.

What you want to know from the lender are two things: How much time will you have to flip the property? How much money will it cost to delay the foreclosure sale?

You may have a long-term wealth-building strategy for your abandoned-property investing. In that case, you will have a different conversation with the owner's lender. In fact, you may have to talk to several other lenders.

Speaking of lenders, in the next chapter we will show you the four ways to obtain financing to rehab or hold your abandoned-property investment. These four ways include owner finance, existing lender(s), new lenders, and money partners. What is really fun is the combinations of these four main financial possibilities.

CHAPTER **11**

Four Ways to Obtain Financing to Rehab or Hold Abandoned Property

In this chapter we will show you four ways to obtain financing to rehab or hold your abandoned-property investment. These four ways include owner finance, existing lender(s), new lender(s), and money partners. What is really fun is the combinations of these four financial possibilities.

You can combine owner finance with a new lender. You can combine an existing lender with a money partner. You can combine an existing lender with a new lender. This gives you added flexibility to rehab or hold your abandoned-property investment.

Some of you will have a quick-cash investment strategy to rehab the abandoned property and immediately sell it. Some of you will have a long-term wealth-building investment strategy to rehab the property and hold it. Some of you will decide not to rehab or do not need to rehab the property and just sell it (quick cash). Finally, some of you will decide not to rehab or do not need to rehab the abandoned property and hold on to it (long-term wealth building).

1. Owner Finance/New Lender

We are going to give you a different take on owner finance in this chapter. Most people use owner finance in the context of acquiring a property. In the next chapter, "Creative Financing of Abandoned Property," we will give you that take on owner finance.

For our purposes here, we want to talk about owner finance as it relates to rehabbing an abandoned property. How is it possible to get the abandoned-property owner to help you finance rehabbing their former property?

Owner Finance to Rehab Abandoned Property

We are going to describe how you can make this happen. Then we are going to give you an example from our abandoned-property investing experience. It all begins with writing your foolproof abandoned-property offer.

Your Foolproof Abandoned-Property Offer

As part of building rapport with the abandoned-property owner, we ask lots of questions. We are trying to get the most accurate read on what the abandoned-property owner wants to have happen with their property. We are also trying to find out to what extent they can help us once we make a deal.

The primary motivation for the abandoned-property owner is to salvage whatever equity or financial stake they have in the property. This leads us to a financing technique that puts money in the abandoned-property owner's pocket and gives you money to rehab the property.

Overencumbering

One of the ways an abandoned-property owner can make their property more attractive to buyers is to provide them with allowances to make repairs or improvements to the property. For example, they can give a carpeting allowance or an appliance allowance in the form of cash at closing to the buyer. This may range from as low as $2,000 to $3,000 or as high as $10,000 to $20,000.

We want to give you a different way to do this that will give you the cash you need and enable the abandoned-property owner to receive the most equity out of their property. Again, our purpose here is to give you a way to have money to rehab the property.

When you place a loan on a property, you encumber the title to the property. If the borrower does not pay back the loan, the lender can sell the property to recover their loan proceeds. Typically, the property is worth more than the loan. When the loan(s) is worth more than the property, then the property is said to be overencumbered.

Overencumbering Example

We found an abandoned property that was worth $200,000. There was a relatively small first mortgage of $40,000. The equity position for the abandoned-property owner is $160,000. We had our money partners qualify for and obtain a new first mortgage of $160,000. However, we did not want to put any money into a down payment.

Abandoned-Property Owner's Equity Position

Property Value	$200,000
Existing First Mortgage	−$40,000
Owner's Equity Position	$160,000

We determined that we needed $20,000 to fix up and make improvements in the property. This is how we made the transaction work for us and the abandoned-property owner. Out of the new $160,000 first mortgage, we paid off the abandoned-property owner's first mortgage of $40,000. This left $120,000 in available cash.

Available Cash

Property Value	$200,000
New First Mortgage	$160,000
Existing First Mortgage	−$40,000
Available Cash	$120,000

Out of the $120,000 in available cash, we received $20,000 at the closing so we could rehab the property. This left $100,000 in cash for the abandoned-property owner.

Cash to Abandoned-Property Owner

Available Cash	$120,000
Cash to Rehab Property	−$20,000
Cash to Owner	$100,000

Remember, the abandoned-property owner's equity position is $160,000. If we hadn't received $20,000 to rehab the property, the abandoned-property owner would have received $120,000 cash. Then they could have carried a $40,000 second mortgage from us for the balance of their equity.

However, we did receive $20,000. This $20,000 is a loan from the abandoned-property owner and not a gift. So rather than carrying a $40,000 second mortgage, we had the abandoned-property owner carry a $60,000 second mortgage. Now with the $100,000 cash they received and the $60,000 second mortgage, they reached their $160,000 equity position.

Abandoned-Property Owner's Equity Position

Cash to Owner	$100,000
Second Mortgage	+$60,000
Owner's Equity Position	$160,000

Now the property is overencumbered. There is a new $160,000 first mortgage. There is a $60,000 second mortgage. The property is worth $200,000. The total of the first mortgage and the second mortgage is $220,000!

Property Overencumbered

First Mortgage	$160,000
Second Mortgage	+$60,000
Total Mortgages	$220,000

It is okay that the property is overencumbered. The $20,000 in loan amount beyond the property value is offset by the improvements made by rehabbing the property. Of course, you may want to set up some controls on accessing the $20,000 so the abandoned-property owner feels comfortable.

The $20,000 can be put in an escrow account and released incrementally, like a bank does with a construction loan to a builder. As you present purchase orders and contractor bills, then the escrow releases funds.

Some of you may already be thinking of a way to divide the $60,000 second mortgage into smaller increments. What about a $20,000 second mortgage to secure the $20,000 improvement funds and a $40,000 third mortgage for the balance of your equity position? Just use your imagination and be flexible.

2. Existing Lender/Money Partner

We have combined the existing lender with a money partner on several abandoned-property deals. We have brought in a money partner in combination with assuming the existing loan to provide the money to rehab an abandoned property. We have brought in a money partner in combination with assuming an existing loan to hold an abandoned property.

Money Partners

Now is a good time to talk about money partners. There is a ton of money out there looking for a good real estate investment. Our experience as real estate investors has been finding that the right property and/or the right seller is much harder to find than the right money partner.

If you're the kind of person who has a lot of money to invest in real estate, congratulations! We wish you good luck in finding a good abandoned-property deal. Unless you know value in your target area or you find someone like us in your area, you will wind up paying too much for your properties. Of course, you could always contact us! We do business anywhere!

We have already said, *buy the property first, then get the financing.* Most people think of a money partner as someone who puts up the down payment or can pay all cash for the property. We have used a money partner to do both of these things. Sometimes, finding a money partner is finding someone who will put up his credit or ability to get a real estate loan.

Finding a Money Partner

Chapter 17, "How to Find Motivated Partners," includes finding a money partner. We are going to show you how to use money partners to fund your great abandoned-property deals. You find a great abandoned-property investment. You bring it to your money partners. They fund the investment. You split the profit with your money partners.

3. Money Partner/New Lender

We found a property that had been abandoned by the owner. We felt the value of the property rehabbed was $200,000. The property was in bad shape. We knew we would have to do major work to make the house habitable again.

We bought the property at a foreclosure sale for $79,000. We paid cash at the foreclosure sale. The cash was provided by our money partner. We felt we would need another $40,000 to get the property in some semblance of order. We also got this money from our money partner. We now had $119,000 into the property.

Money in Property

Foreclosure Purchase	$79,000
Rehab Costs	+$40,000
Money in Property	$119,000

We went in and took the house down to the studs. The foundation was a pier and beam on real redwood 2" × 4"s. This was the best part of the house structurally. We removed the carpeting and padding and discovered hardwood floors. This was a plus.

The kitchen needed to be completely remodeled. This included knocking out a wall to create more space. The bathrooms were outdated. The tile on the sinks and bath tubs was green. The toilets would have to go.

We knew $40,000 was not going to get the job done. We estimated that we would need another $15,000. The money partner said no to putting more money into the deal.

FHA 203K

Our solution was fairly creative. We wanted to sell the property to a new retail buyer who would live in the home. This would give us the opportunity to make the biggest profit. We also knew that unless the rehab was completed, the buyer would not be able to obtain new financing to complete their purchase.

This was where the Federal Housing Administration (FHA) 203K lending program came in. This is a program through the Department of Housing and Urban Development (HUD). The program allows the buyer who qualifies to purchase the property and include in the new loan the cost of making necessary repairs and improvements.

An appraisal is performed to determine the value of the property after the rehab is completed. The loan to the buyer is made for an amount that will cover the purchase price and the rehab costs. According to HUD, "The amount of the loan will also include a contingency reserve of 10 percent to 20 percent of the total remodeling costs and is used to cover any extra work not included in the original proposal."

At the closing, we get paid and the remaining loan proceeds are put in an escrow account. Mortgage payments for the buyer and the remodeling begin after the deal closes. Let's see how this worked out for us and the buyer.

The Deal

We agreed to sell the property to the buyer for $200,000. This was the appraised value of the property after the rehab was completed. After the buyer made a 3 percent down payment of $6,000, they would receive loan proceeds of $194,000.

The Deal

Purchase Price	$200,000
Down Payment	−$6,000
Loan Amount	$194,000

We would receive $185,000. This was from the $6,000 down payment and $179,000 of the loan proceeds. The additional $15,000 of the loan would be available in an escrow account for the buyer to complete the remodeling.

Follow the Money

We Received	$185,000
Escrow Account	+$15,000
Total	$200,000

Our Profit

So how did we make out in this money partner/new loan deal? We paid $79,000 for the property at the foreclosure. We put $40,000 into rehabbing the property. This $119,000 was from our money partner. We received $185,000 at the closing. We made $66,000 on this deal. What was great is that we didn't have to come up with the additional $15,000. That would have derailed our deal. Thank you HUD 203K!

Our Profit

Money Received	$185,000
Money in Deal	−$119,000
Our Profit	$66,000

4. Existing Lender/Owner Finance

We found a vacant property that was worth $195,000 to $205,000, depending on its condition. The owners had a mortgage of $157,000, which we planned to take over. They were trying to sell the property for $175,000. The owners told us that if they could get $5,000 cash, they would walk away from the property!

We discovered that the loan payments were current and were $1,200 per month. The property taxes were current, but six months of property taxes were accumulated and amounted to $2,500. We inspected the property and realized we would have to replace the carpeting. This would cost $4,000.

Property Equity

Property Value	$200,000
Mortgage	−$157,000
Property Equity	$43,000

For $5,000 we would have a $43,000 equity position in the property! We went back to the owners and said we would buy their property under the following conditions. We would give them their requested $5,000.

Our Offer

If we were going to give them $5,000, however, we wanted them to compensate us $4,000 for the carpeting, $2,500 for the six months of property taxes that was their responsibility, and $3,600 for the next three mortgage payments.

We explained to the owners that they would be responsible for three mortgage payments if we had a 90-day closing. If they agreed to our offer, we would close in three days. How did the deal look now?

Our Offer

Owner Pays Carpeting	$4,000
Owner Pays Property Taxes	$2,500
Owner Pays Three Months of Payments	+$3,600
Total	$10,100
Buyer Credits Owner	−$5,000
Buyer Receives at Closing	$5,100

The owners paid us $5,100 to make their abandoned-property problem go away. We now had a $43,000 equity position and $5,100 cash in our pockets.

We took the $5,100 and replaced the carpets and repainted the interior of the house. The owner had essentially financed our rehabbing of the property. We then rented the property for $1,950 per month. This gave us a $300 per month positive cash flow.

In the next chapter, we want to give you several examples of how and when to use creative finance. By having the flexibility to use creative finance, you may be able to close an abandoned-property deal that you would miss otherwise.

CHAPTER 12

Creative Financing of Abandoned Property

In this chapter we want to give you several examples of
how and when to use creative finance. By having the flexibility to use creative finance, you may be able to close an
abandoned-property deal that you would otherwise miss.

When you are negotiating an abandoned-property real
estate contract, there are two main negotiating points: price
and terms. You may want to get your price *and* your terms.
That may not be a realistic position to take if you want to
make an abandoned-property deal.

If you get your price, you may want to work with the
abandoned-property owner on their terms. If you get your
terms—say, nothing down—you may want to work with the
abandoned-property owner on their price.

Owner Financing

Owner financing and creative financing go hand in glove. Part
of your job as a real estate investor is to educate owners about
carrying financing for them to make the deal go. You are trying to get across to the abandoned-property owner that their
being flexible will contribute to a successful negotiation.

Second Mortgage

We found an abandoned property that we felt was worth $250,000. The abandoned-property owner agreed to sell us the property for $200,000. We were going to take over their existing first mortgage of $150,000. What was left for us to figure out was how we were going to cover the $50,000 equity position the abandoned-property owner had in the property.

Owner Equity

Purchase Price	$200,000
First Mortgage	−$150,000
Owner Equity	$50,000

At first they insisted that they needed to receive all of their equity in cash. We wanted to put no more than $40,000 in cash into the deal. We wrote our offer to include a $40,000 cash down payment and asked the abandoned-property owner to extend a $10,000 second mortgage.

We presented our offer for $200,000 with us taking over the existing $150,000 first mortgage, making a $40,000 cash down payment, and requesting the owner to carry back a $10,000 second mortgage.

Our Offer

Purchase Price	$200,000
Take Over Existing First Mortgage	$150,000
Cash Down Payment	$40,000
Owner Second Mortgage	$10,000
Owner Receives	$50,000

During the offer presentation we educated the abandoned-property owner on the benefits of carrying back a second mortgage. If they carried back the $10,000 at 7 percent annual interest payable $100 or more monthly and all due in 36 months, they would receive $3,600 in monthly payments. After 36 months they would receive a $9,673 balloon payment. The total they would receive carrying the second would be $13,273.

Owner Receives on Second

Total Monthly Payments	$3,600
Balloon Payment	+$9,673
Owner Receives on Second	$13,273

When we pointed out to the owner that they would effectively receive more than $53,000, we had their interest.

Total Owner Receives

Cash Down Payment	$40,000
Second Mortgage	+$13,273
Total Owner Receives	$53,273

Risk

The owner liked the numbers but wanted to know what their risk would be extending us a second mortgage. Now you are in the education business. We told them we could default. They might have to foreclose on their second mortgage. They wanted to know how that would affect their equity.

We gave them the following scenario. Say we or a buyer we sold the property to defaults on their second mortgage and the first mortgage. The owner forecloses on their second. They wind up getting the property back subject to the remaining balance on the first mortgage.

The property is now worth $210,000. The first mortgage balance is $148,000. They have received $1,200 in monthly payments on the second mortgage. Their foreclosure expenses including bringing the first mortgage current are $3,500. They have received the $40,000 cash down payment. How would they make out?

Owner Forecloses on Second Mortgage

Property Value	$210,000
First Mortgage Balance	−$148,000
Owner Equity Position	$62,000
Received Down Payment	$40,000

Payments Received on Second	+$1,200
Total Gain	$103,200
Foreclosure Expenses	−$3,500
Owner's Net Gain	$99,700

We told them that, not to be mean-spirited, but they could almost be forgiven for hoping we or a buyer we sold the property to defaults on their second mortgage! They would keep the $40,000 down payment plus the 12 months of payments and have an increased equity position when they regain ownership of the property after the foreclosure. Risk? What risk?

We told them the only risk is for them to reject our offer. Three or four months could go by before they get another offer. When it comes in for $190,000, they would jump on it. Besides losing $10,000 in equity, they would be out another $4,500 in mortgage payments, property taxes, and insurance premiums, making their net gain only $36,000. Needless to say, after this presentation they accepted our offer.

Owner Rejects Our Offer

New Purchase Price	$190,000
Additional Payments	$4,500
First Mortgage	−$149,500
Owner's Net Gain	$36,000

Shoe on the Other Foot

Put yourself in the position of having made an abandoned-property deal like we just did in the previous example. Now you are the owner. Would you extend owner financing to make a deal to a new buyer? We hope your answer is yes.

The no-brainer aspect of extending owner financing for part of your equity should now be apparent. By being a flexible seller, you have greatly increased the number of potential buyers for your property. Those inflexible sellers who want all their equity in cash will give you the competitive edge in getting your property sold.

Nothing Down

Let's take a look and see what happens if you sell your property and take all of your equity in mortgage notes. Why would you do this? Perhaps you may not need your equity in cash. Maybe you would like to have a monthly income.

How about you want a better return than putting your cash equity proceeds in the bank? You want the safety of an investment that is secured by real estate. You are unwilling to take the risk of putting your money in the stock market.

Using the numbers we have already become familiar with, let's see what happens if you have a buyer who will pay $200,000 for your property, can afford to make the monthly payments on your $150,000 first mortgage, but has no money for a down payment. Should you automatically reject their offer? No! Let's look at the numbers.

Let's say you carry back the second mortgage for $50,000 at 7 percent annual interest, with monthly payments of $500, all due in 36 months. You would receive $18,000 in monthly payments. You would receive $41,681 as a balloon or final payment. Your total received would be $59,681.

Total Received on Second Mortgage

Monthly Payments	$18,000
Balloon Payment	+$41,681
Total Received on Second Mortgage	$59,681

Now you receive almost $210,000 for your property. Where else are you going to get a 7 percent return on an investment that is secured by real estate?

Received for Property

Assumed First Mortgage	$150,000
Total Received on Second Mortgage	+$59,681
Received for Property	$209,681

Buyer Defaults

To be fair, let's see what happens if the buyer defaults on your second mortgage after 12 months. The buyer also defaults on the first mortgage. You foreclose on your second mortgage. You get the property back subject to the existing loan balance on the first mortgage.

The property is now worth $210,000. The first mortgage balance is now $148,000. You have received $6,000 in monthly payments. Your foreclosure expenses including bringing the first mortgage current are $3,500. How does this turn out for you?

Owner Forecloses on Second Mortgage

Property Value	$210,000
First Mortgage Balance	−$148,000
Owner Equity Position	$62,000
Payments Received on Second	+$6,000
Total Gain	$68,000
Foreclosure Expenses	−$3,500
Owner's Net Gain	$64,500

Split the Notes

What if you are willing to take all of your equity in mortgage notes but want to have the possibility of converting some of that equity to cash before the balloon payments are due? One way you can do this is to split the mortgage notes. Instead of carrying a $50,000 second mortgage on the $200,000 home, as in the previous example, what if you carried a $10,000 second mortgage and a $40,000 third mortgage?

Both the second and third mortgages would have a 7 percent annual interest rate and would be due in 36 months. The second mortgage would have $100 monthly payments. The third mortgage would have $400 monthly payments. So far, this would have the same net result as the $50,000 second mortgage; same interest rate, same due date, same total monthly payment.

Twelve months go by, and you need to get your hands on some quick cash. You will be able to sell the $10,000 second

mortgage, which has a remaining balance of $9,484, for some-
where between $8,000 and $9,000.

Sell $10,000 Second Mortgage

Remaining Balance $9,484

A real estate investor who purchases mortgage notes will
gladly make you an offer on your second mortgage, which has
been seasoned with 12 months of on-time payments. You get
your quick cash for a minimal discount ($400 to $1,400), and
the real estate investor has an 18 percent to 31 percent yield
on his or her investment. (For information on this highly profitable area of real estate investing, see our book *The New Path
to Real Estate Wealth: Earning without Owning* [John Wiley &
Sons, 2003].)

If you were going to sell your $50,000 second mortgage,
you might not be able to find a buyer because the combination of the first and second mortgages would create a loan-
to-value ratio that would be too high. The balance on the
$150,000 first mortgage would be $148,000. The balance on
the $50,000 second mortgage would be $47,400. This would
be a total loan balance of $195,400.

Total Loan Balance

Balance on First Mortgage	$148,000
Balance on Second Mortgage	+$47,400
Total Loan Balance	$195,400

The property is now worth $210,000. This would be a
loan-to-value ratio of 93 percent!

Loan-to-Value Ratio

$195,400 / $210,000 = 93%

There is not enough equity beyond the financing to protect a real estate investor buying the second mortgage. The
buyer of the second mortgage would want no more than an
80 percent investment-to-value ratio.

The investment-to-value ratio is the combination of the
remaining balance on the first mortgage and the amount of

cash they are investing in buying your second mortgage. This would mean that the total of the balance on the first mortgage plus the cash invested in the second mortgage could be no more than $168,000.

Investment-to-Value Ratio

$168,000 / $210,000 = 80\%$

Because the remaining balance on the first mortgage is $148,000, at most you would receive $20,000 cash for your $47,400 equity in your second mortgage.

Cash for Your Second Mortgage

Total Investment-to-Value Ratio	$168,000
Remaining Balance on First Mortgage	−$148,000
Cash for Your Second Mortgage	$20,000

Other Creative Agreements

Buyers and sellers often use agreements in addition to, in combination with, or instead of the purchase offer. For example, an abandoned-property owner may lease their property to you before closing. You may lease the property to the abandoned-property owner after closing. You may lease the abandoned property with an option to buy. The abandoned-property owner may give you just an option to buy.

We have found that when we invest in abandoned property we need to bring our entire real estate contract arsenal with us to the negotiating table. For the rest of this chapter we will present some of the other creative agreements we use in our abandoned-property investing.

Lease

A lease is a contract by which one party (lessor) transfers possession and use of property for a limited, designated term at a specified price and under the stipulated conditions to another party (lessee).

You can buy blank lease forms at your local stationery store or in some states from your Board of Realtors. Books available at your local library or bookstore contain sample leases. Consult with your attorney or real estate professional if you have questions concerning leasing.

The advantage of leasing an abandoned property rather than buying it is it can protect your investment capital. If you lease all or part of an abandoned property after you buy it, then you can obtain income from a property that otherwise might be costing you money to hold on to.

The disadvantage to a lease is that the lessees (renters) may not pay the rent. They can be difficult to remove from the property if there is a problem. Lessees may cause considerable damage before you can remove them from the property.

Option

An option is a contract that gives potential buyers (option-ees) the right to purchase a property before the specified future date for the amount and under the conditions listed in the contract. Also, buyers agree to pay an added amount—an option fee—if they do not use the option.

The seller does not receive money for the sale until the property is sold, usually near or at the end of the option period. Unless you negotiate otherwise, the abandoned-property owner cannot legally raise the property's price during the term of the option.

Some investors recommend using an attorney to draw up the option agreement. We recommend this only if it will make you feel more comfortable or if it is part of a very complex abandoned-property deal. We have found options very useful in investing in abandoned property.

Please see Chapter 16, "How to Option Abandoned Property," for a complete conversation about options. We will mention here that by using an option, the price of the abandoned property can be determined by a mutually acceptable method between us and the abandoned-property owner at the time we exercise the option. This has helped us stay out of some bad deals.

Lease-Purchase Agreements

If *you* lease an abandoned property during the period *before* escrow closes, use a lease in combination with the purchase contract or a consolidated form, such as an interim-occupancy agreement. This gives the abandoned-property owner an income that otherwise might be a help to their cash flow. This gives you an opportunity to see things about the property that you do not like. It also may save you from doing a bad deal.

On the other hand, if you are leasing the property, you may have difficulty getting buyers to vacate the property if they refuse to go through with the sale. Buyers who refuse to complete the sale might cause considerable damage before you can remove them.

Sale-Leaseback Agreement

If you rent or lease the abandoned property to the abandoned-property owner after escrow closes, use a lease in combination with a purchase contract or a specific sale-leaseback form, such as an interim-occupancy agreement. This may also work in combination with an equity-share agreement between you and the abandoned-property owner.

Equity Share
They may have moved out of the property fearing a foreclosure. By putting an equity-share deal together with you, they may move back into the property. In return for you making up the back mortgage payments, you get a 50 percent ownership interest in the property.

Lease Option

If you agree to lease your property with an option to buy, use a lease option or a combination of a lease, an option, and a purchase contract. This enables you to obtain income from a property that otherwise might be costing you money. If the buyers do not exercise the option, you get to keep the option fee.

Your buyers can decide to purchase your property at any time within the lease period. You do not receive money for the sale until the property is sold, usually near or at the end of the lease period. Unless you negotiate otherwise, you cannot legally increase the property price during the contract.

Remember, after the buyers live in the property, they may discover certain inconveniences or problems that they did not expect. This may lead them to want only to live in the property and not to purchase the property.

Points to Consider
If you decide to use a lease option, think about requesting approval for the lease option from an existing lender. The loan may contain a due-on-sale clause that could be triggered by a lease option. Include a provision for buyers to forfeit their security deposit if they decide not to purchase the property on a lease option. Add a clause for buyers to make monthly lease payments that equal or exceed payments on the existing loan. You may want to insert a provision that you credit buyers with a portion of the monthly lease payment toward the purchase price.

Reverse-Lease Option (Sale Leaseback with Option to Purchase)

As a final creative solution, we give you the reverse-lease option. When we think of lease options, we think of leasing the property with an option to purchase the property at some point in the future at some agreed-upon price.

An abandoned-property sale twist on this technique is to purchase the property and lease it back to the owner. You also give them an option to purchase the property at some point in the future at some agreed-upon price.

The agreed-upon future price should include any cash you put into paying the delinquent mortgage payment and property taxes plus any negative cash flow (if applicable) and an acceptable return on your investment. As with the equity-sharing arrangement, consult your attorney for assistance in structuring the transaction.

Purchase Option

A purchase-option contract states that potential buyers have the right to purchase the property before the specified future date for the amount listed and under the conditions specified in the contract. Also, they agree to pay an option fee that is applied to the purchase price if they exercise the option. If they don't exercise the option, the option fee is forfeited.

If you agree to grant a purchase option, use a purchase-option form or a combination option-and-purchase contract. You cannot increase the price for your property during the term of the contract. A price increase is illegal even if all other properties in the area increase substantially in value.

Our goal for this chapter has been to have you think creatively about structuring your abandoned-property deals. Creative finance may be the only way to put together a win-win abandoned-property deal. Your job is to educate the abandoned-property owner on the creative financing that will be to their and your overall financial benefit.

However creatively you structure your deal, one thing never changes. You must be able to get clear and marketable title to the abandoned property. A clear title is a marketable title. In the next chapter, we will show you how to go about acquiring clear and marketable title for your abandoned property.

CHAPTER 13

Abandoned-Property Investment Strategies

There are two abandoned-property investment strategies that we are going to share with you. The first is the quick-cash strategy. The second is the long-term wealth-building strategy. Each of these abandoned-property investment strategies has its advantages.

The quick-cash strategy is used by abandoned-property investors who primarily like to flip property. The quick-cash strategy has you get into an abandoned-property investment and get out quickly. Hopefully, you have made a quick profit.

The long-term wealth-building strategy is used by abandoned-property investors who primarily like to hold property for income and appreciation. The long-term wealth-building strategy has you get into an abandoned property, rehab it, and rent it.

Quick-Cash Strategy

We primarily use a quick-cash strategy to make money in abandoned property. Another name for the quick-cash strategy is flipping. Flipping is the fastest way to make money in real estate. When you flip a property, you get in and out of a property in a short period of time.

Investing in abandoned property can be very cash intensive. If the abandoned property is a foreclosure, you buy on the courthouse steps and must pay cash. There usually are fix-up expenses or rehab costs with abandoned property that require cash outlays.

There may be carrying costs like mortgage payments, property taxes, and homeowner's association fees. You may have to flip your abandoned property so you can get your cash out in order to be able to go in on another abandoned-property deal.

Top 10 Advantages of the Quick-Cash Strategy

We are going to give you the top 10 advantages when you use the quick-cash strategy. The quick-cash strategy is especially useful for abandoned-property investing. We like quick cash—flipping—because we don't like landlording (we've tried it), we love the art of the deal (flipping allows you to make lots of deals), and we like making money right away.

10. No Income-Tax Problems

One of the major advantages of the quick-cash strategy is you avoid income-tax problems. When you hold rental real estate, it is very easy to recapture depreciation when you sell the property. Currently, if you have recapture of depreciation you pay 25 percent in taxes. How easy is it to recapture depreciation? Just own rental real estate and take depreciation.

9. No Extensive Record Keeping

Can you say *certified public accountant?* When you own rental real estate you must keep extensive records. You will have a full-time job as a CPA, or you will be paying a CPA.

You will have rent receipts. Security-deposit receipts. Checkbooks (notice we used the plural here). You will have checking accounts to reconcile. How about the legal requirement in some areas of having a trust account for tenant security deposits?

You will keep maintenance records. You may have employees with all the paperwork and tax nightmares that entails. Worker's compensation insurance, unemployment insurance, health insurance, Occupational Safety and Hazards Association (OSHA), Social Security taxes, withholding federal income taxes. The list goes on and on.

8. No Lawsuits

Seriously, if you own real property, there is a very high probability that you will be sued. If not by one of your tenants or guests, then certainly by a cutthroat attorney who looks up your real estate holdings in the public record to determine if they will take a case based on the real estate assets you own that they can go after.

When you own property, you are a target for frivolous lawsuits. Some of you reading this know exactly what we are talking about. You have been sued for no apparent reason. We also know that some of you have paid legal settlements just to make the frivolous lawsuits go away.

What is our solution? Don't own real property. Control real property. How do you control real property and not own real property? That is a good question. That is what the quick-cash strategy is all about!

7. No Homeowner's Association

If you are or have ever been part of a homeowner's association, then you know the frustration of dealing with mini-tyrants. Not to mention the $200, $300, or $400 monthly dues.

Or special assessments for painting, landscaping, or roofing in the thousands of dollars. And, if you don't pay your monthly dues or special assessments, then your friendly homeowner's association can foreclose on you and/or sue you.

Homeowner's associations are no longer just attached to condominiums or townhouses. We are seeing more and more maintenance associations attached to planned unit developments (PUDs) and single-family residences (houses).

6. No Repairs and Maintenance Costs

We are sure you have heard the expression *deferred maintenance*. Deferred maintenance is the polite way of saying a property is a fixer-upper because the property owner spent no money on regular maintenance through the years. When a property is in foreclosure, you can bet the last thing the property owner is going to spend money on is repairs and maintenance.

New roof: $10,500. New dishwasher: $425. Gardner: $125 per month. Pool maintenance: $175 per month. Real estate ownership entails significant repairs and maintenance costs. Flipping property helps you avoid these costs.

5. No Hazard Insurance

No fire insurance, no liability insurance, no earthquake insurance. No insurance, period. The last time we checked, any kind of hazard insurance is expensive, and real estate lenders calculate a monthly insurance payment when qualifying you for a real estate loan, even when you prepay the insurance premium in an escrow account for the next year.

4. No Property Taxes

Depending on your state, you may pay property taxes once a year or perhaps twice a year. In states like Texas, where there is no state income tax, property taxes can be quite substantial on even modest properties.

On a property valued by the county tax assessor in our area at $167,000, the annual property-tax bill can amount to $6,600! If you calculate that on a monthly basis, you are paying $550 per month for every month you own the property.

Monthly Property Taxes

Annual Property Taxes	$6,600
Monthly Property Taxes	$550

3. No Monthly Mortgage Payments

Month in and month out, 12 months per year for 30 years. That's 360 payments. Let's look at an example. A $400,000 loan for 30 years at 7 percent interest is payable at $2,661.21 per month including principal and interest. Multiply the monthly payment by 360 payments and you will pay almost $1 million!

Monthly Payments

Monthly Payment	$2,661.21
30 Years	×360
Total of Payments	$958,035.59

The really nauseating number is when you realize that you originally borrowed $400,000! You wind up paying $558,035.59 in interest. That is 140 percent of the amount you borrowed.

Amount of Interest

Total of Payments	$958,035.59
Amount Borrowed	−$400,000.00
Amount of Interest	$558,035.59

2. No Landlording

Do we really have to tell you our landlording horror stories? Do you really think you can be a successful landlord? Being a landlord is a heartless, thankless job. No matter what you do, you are wrong.

1. Quick Cash

And the number-one advantage of the quick-cash strategy is quick cash. Cash is king! Long live the king! The problem with real estate investing for most people is that it takes too damn long to make any money. Yes, we know that if you bought a property on the East Coast or West Coast five years ago you doubled your money. But who has the time or the patience to wait? We don't. Do you?

Flipping is your answer. When you are a real estate investor whose strategy is quick cash, patience does not have to be one of your strengths. In fact, impatience becomes one of your strengths! You become impatient with the deal you are working on and want to get it done so you can get on to the next deal.

The more abandoned-property deals you get involved with, the more money you will make. Although the quick-cash strategy brings you quick cash, unless you are disciplined enough to save or reinvest some of your quick cash, it will disappear as quickly as it came.

Long-Term Wealth-Building Strategy

Some abandoned-property investors employ the real estate investment strategy of long-term wealth building. In long-term wealth building, you buy and hold property for income and appreciation. This can be a very effective strategy in areas of the country that experience very high rates of price appreciation such as California and the Northeast.

We know some of you will prefer using a long-term wealth-building strategy to make money investing in abandoned property. Another way to describe the long-term wealth-building strategy is buying and holding property for income and appreciation.

Top 10 Advantages of Long-Term Wealth Building

We are going to give you the top 10 advantages when using the long-term wealth-building strategy. The long-term wealth-building strategy is also useful for abandoned-property investing. Although we prefer the quick-cash strategy, you may want to buy and hold your abandoned properties. This may be dependent upon in what area of the country you are making your investments.

10. Depreciation

There are income-tax advantages for real estate investors who materially participate in the management of their rental properties. You are able to take depreciation on the improvements and use this depreciation to offset the income the property produces.

Let's say you receive $2,300 in monthly rent for 12 months. This is $27,600 in yearly income. If you are able to take $10,000 in annual depreciation, then you will only have to pay taxes on $17,600 in yearly income.

Yearly Income	$27,600
Annual Depreciation	−$10,000
Taxable Income	$17,600

9. Rehabbing

Rehabbing can be an important component in the value of a property. Real estate investors who rehab an abandoned property contribute not only to their own bottom line but also to the value of the surrounding community.

A property that is rehabbed generates $2 to $3 for every dollar spent rehabbing when you sell the property down the road. If you put $25,000 into rehabbing a property, you can count on a $50,000 to $75,000 value increase as long as you stay within market values for the area where the property is located.

Rehab Amount	<$25,000>
Value Increase	+$75,000
Profit	$50,000

8. Deductibility of Property Taxes

All of the property taxes you pay on the property are tax deductible. When you pay the property taxes, you are able to use this to offset the income the property produces.

Let's say you receive $2,300 in monthly rent for 12 months. This is $27,600 in yearly income. If you pay $5,000 in property taxes, you will have to pay tax on only $22,600 in yearly income.

Yearly Income	$27,600
Property Taxes	−$5,000
Taxable Income	$22,600

7. Deductibility of Mortgage Interest

All of the mortgage interest you pay on the mortgages you used to purchase the property is tax deductible. You are able to use the mortgage interest you pay to offset the income the property produces.

Let's say you receive $2,300 in monthly rent for 12 months. This is $27,600 in yearly income. If you pay $18,000 in mortgage interest, then you will have to pay tax on only $9,600 in yearly income.

Yearly Income	$27,600
Mortgage Interest	−$18,000
Taxable Income	$9,600

If we put depreciation, property tax, and mortgage interest deductibility together from our examples, we would have $10,000, $5,000, and $18,000 respectively. This totals $33,000.

Annual Depreciation	$10,000
Property Taxes	$5,000
Mortgage Interest	+$18,000
Total Deduction	$33,000

This easily offsets our $27,600 in rental income. In fact, the $5,400 excess deduction may be used to offset other income. Check with your tax adviser.

Yearly Income	$27,600
Total Deduction	<$33,000>
Excess Deduction	<$5,400>

6. Long-Term Capital Gains

You receive long-term capital gains tax treatment for property held more than one year. This can be a huge tax savings compared to being taxed at ordinary income-tax rates. Comparing an ordinary income-tax rate of 28 percent with a long-term capital gains rate of 15 percent, you can see that you practically cut your tax bill in half.

Let's say you have a profit of $100,000. At a 28 percent ordinary income-tax rate, you would pay $28,000 in income tax. At a 15 percent long-term capital gains rate you would pay $15,000 in income tax. You save $13,000 in taxes.

Ordinary Income-Tax Rate (28%)	$28,000
Capital Gains Tax Rate (15%)	−$15,000
Tax Savings	$13,000

5. 1031 Tax-Deferred Exchanges

You can defer income-tax consequences by doing a 1031 tax-deferred exchange. Even with favorable long-term capital gains treatment, your tax bill can still be quite substantial.

Let's say you have a long-term capital gain of $400,000. At a 15 percent long-term capital gain tax rate your tax bill will be $60,000 if you sell the property.

Long-Term Capital Gain	$400,000
Long-Term Capital Gains Tax Rate	×15%
Taxes You Owe	$60,000

By doing a 1031 tax-deferred exchange, you will defer having the $400,000 long-term gain recognized. Because the gain is not recognized, there is no tax consequence to you at the time of the sale. You have an additional $60,000 in your pocket to make another real estate investment.

4. Economies of Scale

A nice advantage of long-term wealth building is being able to use the economies of scale as a landlord. When you have accumulated 5, 10, or 15 properties, you can begin a cookie-cutter property-management style.

If there is a sale on paint, you buy paint for all your properties. If there is a sale on carpeting or flooring, you buy carpeting or flooring for all your properties. By buying in bulk, you save money. It is like buying wholesale instead of retail.

3. Cash Flow

People who use the long-term wealth-building strategy want to build in cash flow for any properties they are going to keep. Cash flow contributes to your overall bottom line.

When your income exceeds your expenses, you have positive cash flow. This is a good thing. When your expenses exceed your income, you have negative cash flow, which is, of course, a bad thing.

2. Appreciation

When the market is hot, the market is hot! Our friend John bought a two-bedroom, one-bathroom home in California in 1998 for $420,000 that is now worth $1 million. Every real estate market appreciates. Some markets appreciate at a much higher rate than others. Take a look at the net differences between these various market appreciation rates.

If you are in a market that appreciates at 4 percent annually, property values will double every 18 years. If you are in a market that appreciates at 7 percent annually, property values will double every 10 years. If you are in a market that appreciates at 12 percent annually, property values will double every six years.

Consider what your investment goals are when choosing the market area for your long-term wealth building.

1. Long-Term Wealth Building

And the number-one advantage of the long-term wealth-building strategy is long-term wealth building. You are building a future nest egg by using this strategy. By holding property, you are compounding your equity year after year without any income-tax consequence.

The future is going to come no matter which investment strategy you choose. You must decide if long-term wealth building or quick cash will work best to accomplish your abandoned-property goals. Once you invest your money in abandoned property, it can be difficult to liquidate, or sell, your assets quickly.

Because real estate is the biggest-ticket item there is, there are the fewest buyers in the marketplace compared to any other commodity. The quick-cash strategy addresses the problem historically associated with real estate investing: the lack of liquidity.

In the next chapter, we will show you how to assign your abandoned-property deals. Our number-one way we flip abandoned property is through assigning real estate contracts. This is a way to flip real estate without buying or owning the property. This is one of the ways we use the quick-cash strategy in our abandoned-property investing.

CHAPTER 14

Assigning Your Abandoned-Property Deals

Our number-one way we flip abandoned property is through assigning real estate contracts. This is a way to flip real estate without buying or owning the property. You may not even have to close escrow. We really are not flipping real estate at all. To flip real estate, technically, you need to *own* the real estate.

We are flipping real estate *contracts.* Real estate contracts are personal property. We own the contracts. Once you know how to assign contracts, your real estate investing career is going to take off.

We will give you the information you need to understand assigning contracts. We will talk about the types of contracts you can assign. We will then apply assigning to the abandoned-property arena and show you how to make quick cash assigning your abandoned-property contracts.

What Is Assigning?

Assigning a real estate contract transfers your position in the contract to another person for a fee. Said technically, assigning a real estate contract allows you, the assignor, to assign the contract to a new person, the assignee. An assignment transfers your rights to purchase a property under the terms of a real estate purchase contract to a new buyer.

The new buyer literally steps into your shoes and can buy the property under the same terms and conditions you negotiated with the seller. The assignor gives paperwork, the assignment, to the assignee, who receives the paperwork in return for money or other valuable consideration.

Assignment Fees

The money you receive for assigning a contract is called an assignment fee. The fee is negotiable between you, the assignor, and the person you assign the contract to, the assignee. The other party to the contract you have had accepted—seller, abandoned-property owner, lessor, optionor, lender, or whomever—has no say so in your negotiations with your assignee.

What kind of dollar amount should the fee be that you receive for assigning a contract? We have assigned a contract for as little as $1,000. We have also assigned a contract for as much as $100,000. Typically, the fees we have received for assigning contracts range between $5,000 and $15,000.

Types of Real Estate Contracts that You Can Assign

Virtually every type of real estate contract can be assigned. You can assign purchase contracts, options, leases, lease options, mortgage contracts, trust deeds, the list goes on. You can even assign an assignment contract! If it is a real estate contract, you can figure out a way to assign it. Assigning a contract is the easiest and quickest way to flip real estate.

Purchase Contracts

The complete name for this contract is actually purchase contract for real estate and deposit receipt. This is the contract that contains the terms and conditions to which you and the seller agree when the seller accepts your offer to purchase their property.

You can access the Texas Real Estate Commission's contract at www.trec.state.tx.us. Office-supply stores in your area may carry a generic real estate purchase contract, or you can use a purchase contract from a local real estate company.

The truth of the matter is that you can use a napkin at a restaurant to write a real estate offer. We don't recommend using napkins to write your offers, however; the ink runs on the napkin when it gets wet. (We've had it happen.) As long as the purchase contract is in writing, it is valid. Every state has a statute of frauds, which says for a real estate contract to be valid, it must be in writing.

If you are working with a real estate agent and they want to use their contract, then use their contract. It is not worth the aggravation spending the time to educate a real estate agent on why you should use your contract. Just make sure everything you want in the contract is communicated by whatever purchase contract you use.

You'll want to include everything you can possibly think of in your purchase contract. Every blank space is either filled in, or the letters *NA* (not applicable) are written. You are negotiating not just for yourself but also for the buyer you are going to assign the contract to.

Believe us when we tell you the new buyer wants a really good deal! How the new buyer gets a really good deal is when you write a really good contract that is accepted by the abandoned-property owner.

Your state may require special wording if you are purchasing a homeowner's equity in preforeclosure. Remember, the preforeclosure phase lasts until the foreclosure sale occurs, no matter what state the property is in.

Deposit Receipt

There is a deposit-receipt section in every real estate purchase contract. Sometimes this is referred to as the earnest money deposit. This is where the buyer includes some type of valuable consideration with the contract to show good faith to the seller. In other words, the deposit the buyer attaches to the offer shows that they are earnest about buying the property.

We recommend you use a promissory note as your deposit instrument for all your contracts. We recommend you use a promissory note for two reasons. First, by using a promissory note you protect your cash. Second, you don't want 10, 15, or 20 personal checks out there accompanying all those abandoned-property offers you are writing and presenting.

You only have to turn the promissory note into cash if your offer is accepted and you are going to open an escrow. If you assign your purchase contract before you open escrow, then the promissory note never gets cashed.

The promissory note we recommend you use is in the format of a check. You may be able to find a similar promissory note in the legal-forms section of an office-supply store.

This is a much simpler version than the promissory note used by lenders as evidence of the debt for a real estate loan. The main idea here is to have something attached to the purchase contract that represents consideration. This gives validity to your contract.

Option Contracts

A real estate option contract says you will buy a property within a certain time frame. You will commit funds in the form of an option fee or option money to keep the option open for the period of time agreed on.

Option contracts have a unique feature among all the different real estate contracts. All contracts are bilateral to begin with. Consent in the form of mutual agreement on both the seller's part and the buyer's part is necessary for validity. Once the option has been agreed to, only the buyer can exercise it.

The seller can't back out of the deal if the buyer exercises the option. The optionee (buyer) can back out of the deal and not be sued for specific performance. The optionor (seller) gets to keep the option fee the optionee put up, but that's all.

We use an option contract that is designed to be assigned by the wording of the contract itself. See our book *The New Path to Real Estate Wealth: Earning Without Owning* (John Wiley & Sons, 2003) for a copy of this option contract. In the event you are using an option contract that is not set up to be assigned, all you have to do is add the words *and/or assigns* to the buyer's name portion of the contract.

Leases, Lease Options, Mortgage Contracts, Trust Deeds

Every type of real estate contract can be assigned. Leases, lease options, mortgage contracts, and trust deeds can be assigned. Even an assignment contract can be assigned.

Car dealers use assignments in their rebate programs. Assigning contracts is everywhere in the business world. The point is, we want you to feel comfortable assigning real estate contracts.

How to Assign a Contract

Assigning a contract begins when you write the initial offer. In the initial offer you make to the abandoned-property owner, whether it is a purchase contract, an option contract, a mortgage contract, or a trust deed, you use the terminology *and/or assigns* in the contract.

You have a new name from this day forth. Think of it as if you are being given a royal title. This title is much better than *sir* or *madam*. It is even better than *your royal highness*. It is more powerful than *your majesty*. From now on, as a real estate investor writing contracts, you will be known as *your name and/or assigns*.

Assignment Contract

We have shown you how to assign a real estate contract using the *and/or assigns* name addition. What about an actual assignment contract? We find that having an assignment contract available makes assigning any contract a more viable option.

ASSIGNMENT OF CONTRACT

Date: _____

Owner: _____   Original Buyer: _____
Address: _____   Address: _____
_____   _____

Telephone: _____   Telephone: _____
Fax Line: _____   Fax Line: _____
Cell Line: _____   Cell Line: _____
E-Mail: _____   E-Mail: _____

New Buyer: _____
Address: _____
_____

Telephone: _____
Fax Line: _____
Cell Line: _____
E-Mail: _____

Contract Date: _____
Property Address: _____
_____

_____ (Original Buyer) hereby exercises their unqualified right to assign all their rights, obligations, and responsibilities in the above noted Contract dated _____, with _____ (Owner) to _____ (New Buyer). The new buyer of this property hereby agrees to fulfill all of the same terms and conditions of the above referenced Contract, including all closing requirements as originally stated.

The total consideration for this Assignment payable from the New Buyer to the Original Buyer shall be: _____ dollars ($), payable at _____ in the form of a Cashier's Check as of the date of the execution of this Assignment of Contract.

Original Buyer: _____   New Buyer: _____
_____   _____
Date: _____   Date: _____

You still want *and/or assigns* in the buyer's name section in whatever contract you are writing. By using the assignment contract in conjunction with *and/or assigns,* you build an added layer of written protection for yourself, the owner of the property, and the new buyer.

Assigning a contract is completely aboveboard and legal. When an abandoned-property owner asks you what *and/or assigns* means, this is what you should say:

And/Or Assigns Script

"_____ (abandoned-property owner's name), the *and/or assigns* clause gives both you and us the added flexibility to bring in additional buyers or money partners to successfully close our transaction. Would that be all right with you?"

In our experience, the abandoned-property owner's answer has always been yes. Sometimes we have had to work a while with the abandoned-property owner and educate them on the benefits that this phrase has for them. All you are trying to do with *and/or assigns* is create flexibility.

Abandoned-Property Owner Says No

What do you do if the abandoned-property owner's answer is no? You want to make sure they understand what you are trying to do by having the ability to assign your contract. Flexibility is the name of the game in making an abandoned-property deal work.

Flexibility on your part and the abandoned-property owner's part is especially important in a preforeclosure abandoned-property deal. If they will not agree to give you the flexibility you need by having *and/or assigns* in your contract, let them know that you will not proceed to present the rest of the offer.

You must stick to your guns on this point. *And/or assigns* is that important to your abandoned-property investing success. It is much harder to come back to the negotiating table after you have already reached an agreement with the owner. Have *and/or assigns* be part of your agreement from the beginning.

Why Use an Assignment?

There are four main reasons to us an assignment. Assigning a purchase contract makes you money without buying the property. Assigning is the fastest way to flip a property. Assigning is the quickest way to make money in real estate investing. Assigning avoids all the pitfalls of real estate ownership.

Assigning Makes You Money without Buying Property

Assigning a real estate contract makes you money without buying property. In a traditional real estate investment, you (the investor) make money by finding a property, writing and having your offer accepted by the seller, opening and successfully closing an escrow, fixing up the property (if necessary), and then selling the property to a buyer. This is what a timeline would look like for buying real estate to make money:

Buying Timeline for Buying Real Estate to Make Money

Find Property	Write Offer	Offer Accepted	Open Escrow	Close Escrow	Fix Up	Sell Property
			Spend Money	Spend Money		Make Money

We are being rather generous with the timeline. It is actually harder than that. The reality of making money when you buy real estate the traditional way begins with that timeline. You really don't make any money until you do the following: advertise and show the property, receive and accept an offer, and open and close an escrow. Then, and only then, do you make money.

Selling Timeline for Buying Real Estate to Make Money

Advertise Property	Show Property	Receive Offer	Accept Offer	Open Escrow	Close Escrow
Spend Money					Make Money

Assigning Is the Fastest Way to Flip Property

Assigning a real estate contract is the fastest way to flip property. Let's face it. Paperwork is the name of the game in real estate investing. The less paperwork involved in a real estate transaction, the better.

The less paperwork involved in a real estate transaction means the less time it takes to complete the transaction. The less time involved on your part and on the part of the real estate investor or retail buyer you are assigning the contract to means a faster turnaround time for you.

Paperwork for Flip without Escrow

This is the paperwork involved in the simplest flip we do. This is a no-money-down deal. There is no escrow involved. We write a purchase contract and promissory note, which we present to the abandoned-property owner. They accept our offer. They give us back our promissory note and a quitclaim deed to transfer title to the property. This makes three distinct pieces of paperwork for the buying side.

Flip Paperwork for Buying Property

1. Real Estate Purchase Contract
2. Promissory Note
3. Quitclaim Deed

We receive a purchase contract and a personal check as an earnest-money deposit from an investor we flip the property to. We give the real estate investor a quitclaim deed.

The investor gives us a cashier's check. We give the investor back their personal check. Again, we don't have an escrow between the investor and us. We have an additional four distinct pieces of paperwork on the selling side.

Flip Paperwork for Selling Side

1. Real Estate Purchase Contract
2. Personal Check
3. Quitclaim Deed
4. Cashier's Check

Now we have a total of seven distinct pieces of paperwork involved in this transaction. There are three pieces of paperwork on the buying side. There are four pieces of paper on the selling side.

Paperwork for Assignment

What if we were able to have just assigned our abandoned-property purchase contract instead of doing a traditional flip in which we actually owned something? Would we speed up the flip by doing an assignment? How much paperwork is involved if we assign our purchase contract?

We write a purchase contract and a promissory note, which we present to the abandoned-property owner. The owner gives us back our promissory note. So far everything is the same as doing a flip.

Here is where the assignment transaction changes the paperwork. The abandoned-property owner does not give us a quitclaim deed. They give a quitclaim deed to transfer title to the investor to whom we assign the purchase contract. We now have one less quitclaim deed using the assignment.

The next paperwork that changes with the assignment is the elimination of the second purchase contract. We do not receive a purchase contract from the investor. The investor takes over our position in the first purchase contract.

The investor does not write a personal check to accompany their offer to us. We receive a cashier's check from the investor. The investor receives the quitclaim deed from the abandoned-property owner.

Assignment Paperwork

1. Real Estate Purchase Contract
2. Promissory Note
3. Quitclaim Deed
4. Cashier's Check

The difference in the amount of paperwork for a flip and an assignment is substantial. The flip paperwork runs to seven items. The assignment paperwork runs to four items.

Our point is that assigning a contract is the fastest way to flip abandoned property. Assigning a contract is flipping property! Flipping is good. When you use assigning as a flipping tactic, you'll streamline the paperwork and reduce the time involved in the transaction. You'll also make the same amount of money on the deal.

Assigning Is the Quickest Way to Make Money

Assigning a real estate contract is the fastest way to make money in real estate investing. When you have a quick-cash strategy, time is definitely of the essence.

The timeline for assigning contracts is substantially shorter than the timeline for a traditional real estate investment. Even with flipping a property, you can't make money as quickly as when you assign contracts.

As you can see, you can make money quicker and at more junctures along the way than with a traditional real estate investment strategy of buy the property, own the property, and sell the property.

Assigning Timeline

Assigning Contracts to Make Money

Find Property	Write Offer	Offer Accepted	Open Escrow	Close escrow	Fix Up	Sell Property
	Make Money	Make Money	Make Money	Make Money		

Assigning Avoids the Pitfalls of Real Estate Ownership

Assigning a contract avoids all the pitfalls of real estate ownership. We feel that assigning is a good strategy for the abandoned-property arena. Assigning abandoned-property contracts has multiple advantages to the traditional buy-and-hold abandoned-property investment strategy.

These advantages include no rehabbing, no landlording, no monthly mortgage payments, no property taxes, no hazard insurance, no maintenance costs, no homeowner's association dues, no lawsuits, no extensive record keeping, and no income-tax problems.

When to Assign a Contract

You can assign a real estate contact before, during, or after the closing. Assigning a contract before the closing is the way we like to do our abandoned-property transactions. You tie up an abandoned property with an accepted contract and immediately search for a buyer to whom to assign the contract.

Assigning a contract during the closing is our second favorite way we like to do our transactions. You tie up the property and assign the contract before the closing takes place. The assignee takes your place in the closing and then winds up closing the escrow.

Assigning after the closing is the final way we like to do our transactions. Again, you tie up a property with an assignment clause in the contract. If you don't find a buyer before closing and wind up closing the property yourself, you can quickly transfer your interest in the property to another buyer after closing. Essentially, you are going to flip the property using what we call an assignment deed.

Look at the timeline for assigning contracts. This will give you a way to visualize the different times you can use an assignment. Anytime you can assign a contract and make money is a good time to do an assignment.

The timeline is the same for assigning in the abandoned-property arena. You can assign your contract after you write the offer to buy the owner's equity and before an escrow is opened. You can assign your contract to buy the owner's equity during the escrow. And you can assign your contract to buy the owner's equity after closing escrow.

Timeline for Assigning Contracts

Write Offer	Open Escrow	Close Escrow
Assign before Closing	Assign during Closing	Assign after Closing

Assignment before Closing

We don't ever want to close an escrow. At least not in the traditional way most real estate investors do. We want to "close" our deals in a different way. In the normal course of events, a real estate transaction goes like this.

A real estate investor finds a potential property. The investor writes an offer on the property and presents it to the owner. There is a negotiation back and forth between the owner and the investor. There is an agreement as to price and terms. Then the owner and the investor open an escrow or go to a closing.

Once the escrow is complete, the escrow closes. The owner receives money or other valuable consideration from the investor. The investor receives the title to and possession of the property.

Close by Assigning

We close our deals by assigning our owner-accepted real estate contracts. By using an assignment of contract, we use a one-page escrow instruction between us and the buyer we are assigning the contract to. In the case of an abandoned-property deal, we have the abandoned-property owner give a quitclaim deed to the new buyer.

Assignment during Closing

An assignment during closing is a very common occurrence in our real estate investing. We have said our favorite time period to do an assignment is before closing, but doing an assignment during closing runs a close second.

The difference between assigning before closing and during closing is whether you have formally opened escrow or not. An assignment before closing means you have written an offer and had it accepted but have not opened escrow before you assign the contract. An assignment during closing means you have done all of this *and* opened an escrow.

The new buyer steps into your position as the buyer in the escrow. The assignment fee can come to you through the escrow or outside the escrow. Either way is fine.

An escrow will be opened for two reasons. If the abandoned-property owner requests an escrow, an escrow will be opened. If the new buyer requests an escrow with the owner, an escrow will be opened.

Assignment after Closing

At first blush, it might seem out of place for us to talk about assigning after the closing. As we have taught you to do with every contract you write, however, you used the clause *and/ or assigns* when you wrote the purchase contract.

What do you do if you decide to close the transaction yourself because it is such a good deal or you have not found a new buyer before the closing date arrives?

The fastest way to assign your interest in a property after you have closed escrow is to quitclaim the property to a new buyer. Whatever interest or title you have in the property is transferred to the buyer.

No one but us will tell you that you can assign a piece of real estate after you have closed escrow. We call a quitclaim deed an assignment deed. We use this deed when we want to quickly get out of a property that we wind up owning.

Once you assimilate the assigning tactic into your abandoned-property investing strategy, you will begin to find all kinds of abandoned-property contracts to assign. Abandoned-property contracts to assign will begin to find you. We look to assign every abandoned-property contract we write.

Some of you may want to take possession of the abandoned property you purchase. In the next chapter, we will show you how to rehab an abandoned property. You may want to rehab it so you can flip and make quick cash. You may want to rehab it so you can keep it for income and appreciation as part of a long-term wealth-building strategy.

CHAPTER 15

Rehab Abandoned Property to Create Instant Equity

In this chapter we are going to show you the best way to rehab your abandoned properties. We have made a lot of money rehabbing these properties and reselling them. We have also lost money by rehabbing abandoned properties. We either spent too much money or spent it on the wrong areas.

The key to making money rehabbing abandoned property is where you spend your rehab dollars. Our rule of thumb is you should expect to at minimum double to triple each dollar spent on rehabbing. If you aren't going to be able to at least double to triple your rehab dollars, we recommend you don't do the rehab.

If you spend $20,000 rehabbing an abandoned property, say you need to get at least $60,000 return on those rehab dollars upon resale.

Triple Rehab Dollars

Spend for Rehab	$20,000
Rehab Multiple	×3
Return on Resale	$60,000

Rehabbing

A property that has well-thought-out improvements, is in good repair, and is attractive is going to sell quickly. Every rehab project should be done with an eye to marketing the property. What does the improvement, repair, or attractiveness feature contribute to how the property is going to show?

Make Necessary Improvements

The improvements you make to a property generally add to its value. Our caveat is that the remodeling is done well and is not an overimprovement. The percentage by which the improvement adds to the value of your property depends on the nature of the improvement and your location.

Some improvements are considered more desirable than others, depending on the area of the country, the city, and even the neighborhood in which you live. We are focusing primarily on residential property in this section.

If you are considering making an improvement, be aware that almost any remodeling will cost more money than you planned and take longer than you think. Many improvements will also be less cost-effective than you estimate.

The following list is intended to give you a general idea of the cost-effectiveness of various renovations. The listed improvements are in descending order, with the remodeling yielding the greatest percentage of return listed first and those yielding the least listed last.

Because the same improvement may be considered more desirable in one geographic area than in another, we will not give specific percentages or ranges. You can check with local contractors or building associations for the order and percentage of value that would be added in your area.

Capital Improvements List

Kitchen	Updates and enlargements are usually most cost effective; overimprovement is not.
Bathrooms	Updates or additions are generally most cost-effective; again, overimprovement is not.

Landscaping	A moderate amount of neat-appearing landscaping is usually cost-effective. Large amounts of landscaping may not be cost-effective because of the amount of maintenance they represent to many buyers.
Flooring	Most cost-effective if you choose flooring of moderate quality in a neutral color and pattern.
Family Rooms	A location in the main living area without reducing other valuable space, such as a garage, is usually best.
Energy Saving Equipment	Storm windows are most cost-effective in areas where they substantially reduce heating and cooling costs. Roof and attic fans are most cost-effective in warm and hot areas. Storm doors are usually not cost-effective.
Bedrooms	A well-located extra bedroom in a two- or three-bedroom home is generally most cost-effective. Extra bedrooms in larger homes may even decrease the salability.
Central Air Conditioning	Central air is most cost-effective in areas with warm summers and only then if extra ductwork need not be installed.
Garages and Carports	Garages are usually more cost-effective in colder climates, near the coast, and in more expensive homes. Carports are usually more cost-effective in warmer areas and in less expensive homes.
Wallpaper	Usually most cost-effective if of moderate quality in neutral colors and patterns.
Swimming Pools	Can be somewhat cost-effective in warm or expensive areas. Many buyers do not like the trouble and cost of maintenance or the possible hazard of a pool.
Garage Conversions	Creating a room from a garage is usually not very cost-effective because the conversion makes the house appear strange from the exterior and the room is often poorly located in relation to the rest of the house.

Complete a Capital Improvements Worksheet

Use a capital improvements worksheet to make a plan of improvements you are thinking about doing to the property. Make improvements only if necessary *and* cost-effective. Make sure you understand what contracting out the improvement work may entail before undertaking any projects. Check with your accountant or tax preparer for the current tax status of these improvements as they affect your bottom line.

Contracting Out Work

If you have a contractor perform work on your property, consider taking actions to reduce the number of problems you have and save you time and money. Such preventive actions include:

1. Learning about the work to be done. The more you know about any job, the better your chances are of getting a job done well.
2. Asking for recommendations. Ask others to recommend someone they know does good work or, preferably, someone who did similar work for them satisfactorily, including:
   - Friends, neighbors, and relatives who own property.
   - Real estate professionals and other investors.
   - Contractors who work in related fields.
   - Subcontractors who are not dependent on those contractors for their livelihood.
3. Ask pertinent questions. When you initially contact a contractor, ask:
   - The address of his or her established place of business.
   - What licenses he or she has, including contractor's license and business license.
   - Whether he or she is bonded.
   - How long he or she has been in business.
   - References for where you can inspect his or her work.
   - List of subcontractors and suppliers.
4. Obtain at least three estimates from competing contractors. If the estimates vary substantially, get more estimates.
5. Choose your contractor.

6. Prepare the contract. Prepare a specific and detailed written agreement with your contractor, including:

- Names, addresses, and license numbers.
- Description of the work. Include sketches, plans, and blueprints as well as a list of products and materials, including brand names and model numbers.
- Dates. Include starting date, 20-day notice date, and completion date. The 20-day notice is a clause stating that failure to begin work within 20 days of the stated starting date is a violation of the contract and makes the entire contract null and void at your discretion.
- Cost.
- Payment schedule. Include a plan of how much you will pay and when. Consider paying in stages of about 20 percent in each installment at the beginning, the end, and as specified portions of the work are completed.
- Permits and licenses. List permits and licenses and who takes responsibility for obtaining them.
- Guarantees.
- Changes in work. A clause to allow your written request for changes without voiding the entire contract.
- Cleanup. Contractor is responsible for cleaning all debris and removing all excess materials.
- Owner's rights and responsibilities.
- Mechanic's lien laws. Incorporate a statement describing your state's mechanic's lien law.
- Cancellation. Include a clause stating that you have three days after signing the contract in which to cancel it.
- Insurance. Incorporate a statement that the contractor is responsible for worker's compensation and liability insurance for his or her workers, subcontractors, and suppliers.
- Completion bond. Make the statement that the contractor will supply a bond. This bond ensures that if the contractor does not complete the project, an

insurance company will pay for the rest of the work to be done.

- Arbitration. Incorporate a clause providing for arbitration in the case of contract disputes.
- Unconditional lien release (waiver of liens). Make the statement that the contractor will provide you with an unconditional lien release after the job is complete and you have made the final payments. With this document, the contractor waives and releases all his or her mechanic's lien rights, stop-notice rights, notice to withhold rights, bond rights, and any and all claims against your property. Without this release, you could end up paying twice for the work.
- Bankruptcy. Include a clause stating that if the contractor goes bankrupt you are not liable for the contractor's debts.

7. Read the contract thoroughly and understand it well before you sign it.

- Do not sign estimates. Estimates may be worded in a manner that makes them binding contracts.
- Do not make separate agreements with subcontractors or suppliers without checking with your contractor.

8. Ensure the quality of the work by:

- Being on site as much as possible while the contractor is working.
- Checking the work as it is done.
- Informing the contractor of problems with the work immediately and in writing.

9. Obtain a detailed, signed receipt stating the amount paid and what the payment is for each time you pay.

10. Sign the certificate of completion and make the final payment only *after:*

- Work is finished to your satisfaction and according to the terms of the contract.
- All subcontractors, suppliers, and workers are paid.

11. Make final payment.

12. Keep a copy of all documents about the work.

Perform Necessary Repairs

Repairing obvious problems makes your property sellable to a greater number of buyers. If your property has obvious damage that needs repair *and* you are able to fix it at a reasonable cost, repairs are very cost-effective.

Do not attempt to conceal problems by making poor or cosmetic repairs. You may be required to make extensive disclosures to buyers regarding your property. Intentionally or carelessly made errors or omissions in the disclosure may leave you liable to buyers for actual damages. The information your state may require you to disclose includes:

1. Facts that you know about the property.
2. Details you, as a reasonable property owner, should know about the property.
3. A reasonable approximation of facts based on the best information available to you, listed as such.

If you do not contemplate making repairs, proceed directly to the section on enhancing your property's attractiveness. If you plan to hire professional help in making repairs, read the section regarding contracting out work before you choose a contractor.

Complete a Repairs Worksheet

Use a repairs worksheet to help you restore your property to a sound condition by:

1. Taking a worksheet to each area of the property and noting only those items you feel need repair work.
2. Reading the completed list and deciding who will be responsible for ensuring that each task is accomplished.
3. Indicating beside each task the date by which you want the repair accomplished.
4. Indicating beside each task whom you need to contact for the repair and their phone number. If you are repairing the item yourself, indicate the materials you need.

    5. Indicating a cost estimate of the repair.

    6. Checking off each item as it is completed.

Enhance the Property's Attractiveness

Most projects you do to enhance your property's attractiveness are like frosting on a cake. Remember, however, that attractiveness is in the eyes, nose, and ears of the beholder.

Complete an Attractiveness Worksheet

Use an attractiveness worksheet to ensure that you handle items that enhance your property's appeal to potential buyers by:

1. Taking a worksheet to each area of the property and noting only those items you feel need cosmetic work.
2. Reading the completed list and deciding which member of your team is responsible for seeing that each item is accomplished.
3. Indicating by each item by what date you feel it should be completed.
4. Indicating beside each item whom you need to contact and the company's telephone number or the materials you need if you will do the job yourself.
5. Indicating an estimate, as you obtain it, of how much you expect each item to cost.
6. Checking off each item.

The Real World of Rehabbing

We are going to conclude this chapter with some of our experiences in the real world of rehabbing abandoned property. Our purpose here is to get you to think about the dos and don'ts of rehabbing abandoned property. We call this next part "Find, Fix, Flip."

Find, Fix, Flip 1

We found a property that was a three-bedroom, two-bath, 1,900 square foot, single-family residence in a good neighborhood. The owners were in the process of getting a divorce. They had moved out of the property in anticipation of being foreclosed on.

The property was a mess. The roof needed repair. The carpets had to be replaced. The floor coverings were beyond repair. Painting was needed inside and out. The landscaping was early jungle. The pool was a breeding ground for West Nile virus–carrying mosquitoes.

We got the seller's written permission to talk to their lender. We were able to forestall the foreclosure for 60 days. We wrote an offer for 65 percent of what we determined to be the retail value of the property. The retail value is the value a property has for an end user like a homeowner.

We felt the retail value was $135,000. Our offer was for $84,500, all cash at closing. The offer was also contingent on our money partner's approval. If our money partner didn't approve of the deal, we had no deal. The seller accepted our offer with no counteroffer.

Potential Profit

Value of House	$135,000
Purchase Price	− $84,500
Potential Profit	$50,500

We brought in our cleanup crew and in five days had stripped the carpeting and floor coverings, cut back the jungle landscaping, drained and cleaned the pool, and painted the entire interior of the house a warm white. We did nothing about the roof. Our total cost was $2,200. We left the big stuff to the next real estate investor.

Finding a Buyer

We called through our list of real estate investors who liked to do major fix-up. The third real estate investor on our list that we showed the property to wanted to buy it. We had the purchase price of $84,500 plus our fix-up cost of $2,200 in the property for a total of $86,700. We sold the property for $92,500 10 days after we had made our offer to the seller. We got our fix-up cost back plus made $5,800. Not bad for 10 days' work.

Our Profit

Sales Price	$92,500
Purchase Price	$84,500
Fix-Up	−$2,200
Our Profit	$5,800

Follow-Up

The investor we sold the property to put $10,000 more into the property. They repaired the roof, put in new carpet and floor coverings, and painted the exterior of the property. They sold the property within 30 days for $132,000. They got back their money they paid us for the property, their rehab cost, plus made more than $29,000 profit. Silly us. We were scared off by the roof damage. We got a good roofer on our team to make repairs after this deal.

Investor Profit

Sales Price	$132,000
Purchase Price	$92,500
Rehab Costs	−$10,000
Investor Profit	$29,500

Find, Fix, Flip 2

Sometimes a real estate deal gets you more involved in the fix-up phase than you want to be. This can especially be the case with abandoned property. This example is instructive in two ways. It is another example of find, fix, and flip. It is also an example of getting too involved with the fix-up or rehab phase.

We found a property that was headed into foreclosure. It was a four-bedroom, three-bath, 2,700 square foot, single-family home in a good neighborhood. The property was vacant. Again, we wrote our offer for 65 percent of the retail value. We felt the retail value was $200,000. Our offer was for $130,000, all cash.

Potential Profit

Value of House	$200,000
Purchase Price	−$130,000
Potential Profit	$70,000

We felt we were getting a great deal. We thought we would spend $20,000 on the fix-up and sell the property for at least $190,000 to $195,000. We would get our $20,000 fix-up money back plus make at least $40,000. Unfortunately for us, this is not the way this deal turned out.

Our $20,000 fix-up budget blew up in our faces. Once we started tearing up the house, we found mold and dry rot. This was not good. We wound up spending closer to $30,000. Still, we felt we would be all right. We would just make less profit.

At this point in our real estate investing, we were doing the major fix-up. This was the biggest fix-up we had ever done. We would buy the property, do all the fix-up, and then we would sell the property to a retail buyer homeowner. We felt this was the way to go because we would make the most money.

With this property we had gotten into major remodeling. We realized too late that we were no longer real estate investors on this property; rather, we were in the remodeling business. Instead of doing the remodeling for a homeowner who was going to pay us, we were the homeowner!

Problem with the Property

We had another problem with this property. We had one of the best properties in the neighborhood. Ninety-eight percent of the properties in the neighborhood were not as nice and were priced less than the property we were trying to sell.

We first tried to sell the property for $200,000. No offers in 30 days. We lowered the price to $190,000. No offers in two weeks. We lowered the price to $180,000. No offers in two weeks. We were starting to get nervous.

It had taken us 60 days to fix up the property. We were now another 60 days into the mission. We were making payments on the $100,000 first mortgage held by the bank. We were making payments on the $30,000 second mortgage the seller had carried back for six months. We had almost $30,000 out of our pocket in fix-up costs.

We finally sold the property, right at the six-month deadline, for $165,000. We lost money on the deal but felt fortunate that we got back most of the money we had put into the property. Right then and there, we realized we never wanted to be in that position again. We knew real estate investing worked. We knew flipping worked. We decided owning and rehabbing/fixing property didn't work for us.

Our Profit

Sales Price	$165,000
Purchase Price	$130,000
Fix-Up	$30,000
Payments	−$6,600
Our Profit	($1,600)

In the next chapter, we will show you how to option abandoned property. We have found that having the ability to write an option contract to control abandoned property gives you added flexibility in your abandoned-property investing.

CHAPTER 16

How to Option Abandoned Property

In this chapter we will show you how to option abandoned property. We have found that having the ability to write an option contract to control abandoned property gives you added flexibility in your abandoned-property investing.

A real estate option contract gives you the right to buy a property without the obligation of having to buy it. In a normal purchase contract when the buyer and seller have a meeting of the minds and sign it, the buyer must perform and go through with the agreed-on purchase. If the buyer does not perform based on the terms of the contract, the seller can sue the buyer for specific performance.

An option contract allows the buyer and seller to have a meeting of the minds, sign the option contract, and offer the buyer a time-certain (a specific stated time frame) to exercise the option. If the buyer does not exercise the option, the option expires, and the buyer owes no further obligation to the seller.

Put another way, an option contract gives a potential buyer the right to purchase a property before the specified future date in the contract for the amount and under the terms and conditions written in the contract.

Optionor/Optionee

In an option contract, the parties to the contract are the optionor and the optionee. The optionor gives real estate paperwork, the option contract, to the optionee. In return, the optionee gives money to the optionor for granting the option. This is called the option fee. The seller is the optionor. The buyer is the optionee.

Option Fee

The option fee is the consideration given by the optionee to the optionor. This is what satisfies the consideration requirement and makes an option contract valid. As we have said, in return for the option fee, the optionor gives the option to the optionee to purchase the property.

The option fee is usually a percentage of the agreed-on purchase price for the property. This percentage can range from as low as 0.5 percent on a higher-priced property to as much as 10 percent on a lower-priced property. For a $100 million purchase price, the option fee may be $500,000. On a $300,000 purchase price, the option fee may be $30,000.

Option Fee Percentages

$100,000,000	Purchase Price	$300,000
×0.5%	Option Percent	×10%
$500,000	Option Fee	$30,000

The option fee can be applied to the purchase price in the event the optionee exercises the option to purchase. Sometimes the option fee does not apply to the purchase price. This may happen when a second or third option time period is negotiated. We always negotiate the option fee applying to the purchase price. That way, if we exercise the option, we already have past money credited to the deal.

Option Fee Applied to Purchase Price

We made an offer on an abandoned five-bedroom, four-bathroom, 5,000 square foot, single-family home in a great neighborhood. Our offer was in the form of an option contract. We wanted a six-month option period because we were concerned about which way the real estate market was headed.

Were we still in the prosperity phase of the real estate cycle? Or were we headed into a recession? If the real estate market was still going in an upward direction, we would buy the property. If the real estate market was headed in a downward direction, we were not going to buy the property.

We negotiated the option fee to be applied toward the purchase price if we exercised the option. If we did not exercise the option, the abandoned-property owner would keep the option fee. In this case, the option fee was $2,500. Although this was a very small percentage of the $300,000 purchase price, the abandoned-property owner still accepted our contract.

Option Fee

Purchase Price	$300,000
Option Fee	−$2,500
Remaining Balance	$297,500

The abandoned-property owner owned the property free and clear. They lived out of state. They had rented the property for a number of years to one family. When the family moved out, the property remained vacant for two years. That was when we came on the scene.

The property was suffering from deferred maintenance. The property rehabbed would have been worth $400,000. A neighbor had a key, and when we looked at the interior of the property, we estimated that $40,000 would handle fix-up and modernizing the kitchen and baths. We would be able to make $60,000.

Our Profit

Sales Price	$400,000
Purchase Price	$300,000
Rehabbing Costs	−$40,000
Our Profit	$60,000

Two months into our six-month option period, the bottom fell out of the local real estate market. An announcement was made that a military base in the area was going to be closed. Prices immediately dropped 15 percent. This was

$60,000! Now the rehabbed $400,000 property was going to be worth $340,000.

There went our profit. Needless to say, we did not exercise our option. We were out our $2,500 option fee. We saved $40,000 in rehab costs.

New Property Value

Old Property Value	$400,000
Value Loss	−$60,000
New Property Value	$340,000

Option Fee Not Applied to Purchase

It happens more frequently than you might expect that the negotiated option fee does not apply to the purchase price. Home builders often acquire finished lots for construction through option contracts with a real estate developer.

In many cases, the home builder will want to extend the option past the original time period. Let's say the first option period was for six months. An extension could be needed by the home builder because they were unprepared to start building.

To extend the option period for another six months, the developer may require another option fee from the builder. Sometimes the second option period may be extended to a third or even a fourth.

Although the developer may have been willing to apply the first option fee toward the purchase price of the lots, the developer may not be willing to apply any of the other fees to the purchase price once an extension or extensions are agreed to.

Why Use an Option?

When you use a real estate option contract, you can tie up a property without revealing your interest in the property. It gives you the right to buy the property without revealing your identity. Once you close on a property, your name is revealed in the public record as the buyer of the property. You can wait to exercise your option until you have put together all the pieces to your overall real estate plan.

Walt Disney

Walt Disney assembled the property for Walt Disney World in Florida using option contracts. He did not want to tip his hand to the many different property owners from whom he needed to purchase property. If remaining property owners knew he was buying property, they could hold out for a higher price. Disney would have had to pay big bucks once word got out that he wanted to put all the properties together for Walt Disney World.

Ten Reasons to Use an Option Contract

1. Maintain Privacy
If it was good enough for Walt Disney, it's good enough for us. As we have said, when you close escrow on a property, the grant deed or warranty deed is recorded. This deed becomes part of the public record. This means anyone in the world can get on the Internet and find out who owns that property. Why? Because the deed names the grantor, the seller, and the grantee, the buyer—that's you.

2. Protect Your Cash
Just like with the stock market, where you can protect your cash by using a stock option, using a real estate option protects the amount of cash you have in any single investment. Rather than buying property with 100 percent of your cash, by using an option you control 100 percent of the property with only a small percentage of the cash.

3. Limited Risk/High Return
Using an option contract limits your risk as an investor and gives you a high return. Leverage has always been one of the benefits of real estate investing. If you think the investment

return is good using the leverage available in a standard real estate transaction, how good do you think the investment return is using an option?

What would the return on our investment be if we used a $20,000 option to tie up a $200,000 property for one year? Let's assume a 5 percent appreciation on the value of the property.

Leverage

Option Fee 10%	$20,000
Purchase Price	$200,000

Appreciation

Purchase Price	$200,000
Annual Appreciation	×5%
Value Increase	$10,000

Return on Investment

Value Increase	$10,000
Amount Invested	$20,000
Investment Return	50%

4. Control Property

The name of the game in real estate investing is control. Donald Trump controls more real estate than he owns. When you have control of something, you are many times in a better position than when you own something. Our abandoned-property investment strategy is based on controlling property, not owning property. We take this one step farther by controlling property with the paperwork of real estate. By using an option contract, you can control lots of abandoned property without owning any of it.

We will briefly mention the advantages of controlling property without owning it. These advantages include quick cash, no landlording, no monthly mortgage payments, no property taxes, no hazard insurance, no maintenance costs, no homeowner's association dues, no lawsuits, no extensive record keeping, and no income-tax problems.

The advantages of controlling property with an option contract are the same as the advantages to flipping property. Except it is better with the option contract because you can flip the contract rather than flipping the property. In other words, with an option contract you control the property without owning it.

Let's add some numbers to this controlling property with options scenario. How much property could you control using $2.4 million as option fees? Some of you can do the numbers in your head. $2.4 million is 10 percent of what number? That's right, $2.4 million is 10 percent of $24 million. No wonder Donald Trump likes to use real estate options.

Leverage

Option Fee 10%	$2,400,000
Purchase Price	$24,000,000

5. Buy Time

By using an option contract you can buy time. You may need time to bring in a money partner. You may need time to get your financing together. You may need time to find a new buyer.

In the time we were writing this book, we found an ad for an abandoned property that was advertised $1 million *under market*. We wrote an offer on the property in the form of a real estate option contract. This was a property we thought about keeping for ourselves.

We will use the option period to find a money partner who will qualify for and obtain a loan to be used to purchase the property. We are planning to assign the option to purchase the property if we decide we are not going to keep the property.

6. Assemble Partners

We use an option contract when we need to assemble partners to go in on a real estate transaction. Sometimes these partners are money partners. Sometimes they are developers. Sometimes they are home builders. Sometimes they are your real estate team for your area.

You may need to find a real estate attorney. You may need an escrow company or closing agent. What about a title insurance company or even a termite company? You may need to find a real estate agent.

Whatever the partnership needs are to put together a successful transaction, by using a real estate option, you will give yourself the necessary time to form the partnership(s).

7. Watch the Direction of the Market

You can use an option to tie up a property and watch the direction of the market. Everyone has 20/20 hindsight with regard to the turning points of the real estate market. The trick is to have 20/20 foresight with regard to these turning points. When things are going well, that is easy to recognize. When things are going not so well, that is easy to recognize.

We have said that the economic cycle is one of expansion, prosperity, recession, and depression. Then it repeats itself. Real estate value is greatly influenced by the economic cycle. Typically, real estate is said to do well in the expansion and prosperity phases and poorly in the recession and depression phases.

8. Handle Contingencies

We use an option contract when we know there are going to be contingencies that need to be handled as part of the purchase contract. A contingency in a contract is a condition that must be met, satisfied, or accomplished, otherwise the whole deal can be blown out of the water.

When you are buying the abandoned-property owner's equity in a preforeclosure situation, you may have to handle several contingencies. Can you take over the existing loan? Will you be able to get clear title? Can you find a buyer to assign the abandoned-property purchase contract to?

We recommend you consider using an option contract to purchase abandoned property. After you have handled all the contingencies, then you exercise your option and purchase the equity.

9. Procure Financing

By using an option contract you can take your time procuring the best available financing for your real estate deal. We have seen interest rates for real estate loans go from historical highs in the early 1980s to historical lows in the early 2000s.

By doing a 6-month, 12-month, 18-month, or even longer option period, you should be able to find an attractive interest rate to finance the transaction. If not, then you do not have to exercise your option.

10. Income-Tax Planning

When you use an option contract you can get certain income-tax advantages as an investor. You may want to use an option contract if you are involved in an Internal Revenue Code section 1031 tax-deferred exchange.

When doing a 1031 exchange, the process sometimes becomes a chicken-and-egg debate. Which comes first? Do you sell the property you have and then look for a property to buy? Or do you find a property to buy and then sell the property you have?

We recommend you "buy" the property you want to exchange into using an option contract. When you find a buyer for the property you are exchanging out of, then you exercise your option and buy the property you want to complete the exchange.

How to Option

Optioning begins with the option contract. You can take a standard purchase contract and turn it into an option contract. Or you can use an option contract from the beginning.

A real estate option contract is similar to a grant deed or warranty deed in that only the seller needs to sign the document to make it valid. Just like in a grant deed or warranty deed, the seller will be granting something in an option contract.

In a grant deed or warranty deed, the seller is granting title or ownership in the property to the buyer. In an option contract, the seller grants the right for the buyer to buy the property during the option period for a price agreed on in the contract.

Option Contracts

We recommend using an option contract from the beginning of the transaction. That way both you and the abandoned-property owner know you are interested in putting together an option at the outset of negotiations.

Memorandum of Option

A memorandum of option can be recorded to protect your optionee interest in the property. Your name as the optionee does not have to appear on the memorandum of option.

If the optionor/abandoned-property owner does try to sell the property to another buyer during your option period, a title company doing a title search for the other buyer will uncover the recorded memorandum of option. This will prevent the abandoned-property owner from transferring clear title, and the deal with the other buyer will fall apart.

Assigning an Option Contract

We use an option contract that is already set up to be assigned by the wording in the contract itself. In the event you are using an option contract that is not set up to be assigned, all you have to do is add the words *and/or assigns* to the buyer's name portion of the contract.

Lease-Option Contract

A lease-option contract can be known by several other names. It may be called a lease with purchase option. It may be called a residential lease with option to purchase. No matter what it is called, its purpose is to combine a lease with an option to purchase.

In a standard lease, the lessor, the property owner, gives a lease to the lessee, the tenant. In return, the lessee pays the lessor rent. In a standard option, the optionor, the property owner, gives an option to the optionee, a potential buyer. In return, the optionee pays the optionor an option fee.

In a lease option, the lessor/optionor, the property owner, gives a lease and an option to the lessee/optionee, the tenant. In return, the lessee/optionee pays the lessor/optionor rent. There is no option fee in addition to the rent.

The lease may require a deposit to be applied to a security deposit, a key deposit, a cleaning deposit, last month's rent, and/or whatever else the landlord wants. These deposits are not an option fee.

When to Option

As we have said, using a real estate option contract you can control property without buying it. In abandoned-property investing, timing is everything. You need to be in the right place at the right time. You also have to use the right investing tools at the right time.

Lawsuits, Creditors, Divorce, IRS Liens

Aside from tipping off surrounding property owners and potential competition, there are four more important situations when it may be in your best interest to use an option contract to protect your privacy. These include being involved in a lawsuit, being hounded by creditors, going through a divorce, and having the IRS on your case.

Lawsuits
When you own real estate, you are a target. Attorneys file lawsuits against people they think have assets worth going after. Attorneys take on clients for a percentage of the money the attorney can win in court.

How many of you have heard the expression "you can't get blood out of a turnip"? When an attorney is searching the public records to find your real estate assets, you want them to think you are a turnip.

Creditors

When creditors come after you, what do they come after? They may not be able to get your home, but they certainly come after your real estate investments. What real estate investments?

Divorce

If your ex-spouse is trying to get money out of you, the first place his or her attorney will look is to your real estate investments. Again, what real estate investments?

IRS Liens

Don't even get us started on the IRS or your state taxing authority. If you don't pay the taxing authority what they think you owe them, they will put tax liens on your real estate assets. When you go to sell these assets, the tax lien will show up against the title to your property.

So if you are involved in one of these situations, we recommend using options. You can be a real estate investor who controls property without owning it. We are firm believers in the right to privacy in business affairs. Make using options part of your privacy protection.

Options and Foreclosure

We are going to conclude this chapter on optioning abandoned property with examples of using an option contract in the foreclosure arena. You may want to use an option to tie up the owner's equity in preforeclosure. You may want to use an option to help an owner get their hands on some cash in return for your having an equity interest in the property. Let's take a look.

In a nonforeclosure situation, if the retail value of the property is $200,000 and the mortgage balance against the property is $140,000, the owner's equity is $60,000.

Nonforeclosure Situation

Retail Value	$200,000
Mortgage	−$140,000
Owner's Equity	$60,000

In a foreclosure situation, the value of a property is no longer the retail value. The property may be run-down. The abandoned-property owner does not have the luxury of a normal marketing time to bring in the highest price. In other words, the value of the property is lowered automatically in a foreclosure situation. Let's say the value of the property is now $185,000 to $190,000.

The mortgage lien goes up in a foreclosure situation. The missed payments are added to the remaining balance of the mortgage. If the missed payments total $10,000, then the mortgage lien is now $150,000.

If the lender has formally initiated the foreclosure process, there are foreclosure expenses added to the mortgage balance. Let's say these foreclosure expenses are $3,000. Now the total mortgage balance is $153,000. Now the abandoned-property owner's equity is substantially reduced.

Please be clear on what we are saying here. The abandoned-property owner has suffered the equity loss. With a new owner back in control of the property, who is not in a foreclosure situation, the value of the property goes back up. When the value of the property goes back up, the owner's equity increases dollar for dollar.

This becomes a negotiating tool for you with the abandoned-property owner. Your point is that the maximum you can offer them is $10,000 cash for their equity. By giving them $10,000 for their equity, you will have $23,000 in the property before you make any money!

We have found that when we show the abandoned-property owner these types of figures, they are much more amenable to accepting our offer. We are not trying to be mean to them or take advantage of them. We are trying to help them. But we (you) can't help them if we (you) can't make any money. Otherwise, we (you) will be in a foreclosure situation ourselves!

Making Money

Speaking of making money, let's look at the numbers. The mortgage balance is back to $140,000 (actually a little lower because the back payments reduced the principal, but really not worth mentioning). The property restored to retail value is now worth $200,000 (or perhaps a bit more).

Retail Buyer

If we sell the property to a retail buyer, we will make a $60,000 gross profit minus the $37,000 invested equals a $23,000 net profit. That is a 62 percent return over perhaps a three-month to six-month time period. That makes the investment worth the risk.

Making Money with a Retail Buyer

Sales Price	$200,000
Mortgage	−$140,000
Gross Profit	$60,000
Money Invested	−$23,000
Net Profit	$37,000

Assign Contract to Wholesale Buyer

If we assign the contract to a real estate investor who rehabs property, we will have no cash to the abandoned-property owner, no cash to the lender, no repairs and fix-up costs, and no carrying and resale costs. Do you think it is possible to flip our contract for $5,000 to $10,000? We did exactly that.

Making Money with a Wholesale Buyer

Assignment Fee	$10,000
Mortgage	−0
Gross Profit	$10,000
Money Invested	−0
Net Profit	$10,000

Tying Up the Abandoned-Property Owner's Equity

In Chapter 9 we talked about buying the abandoned-property owner's equity. We are going to bring back that situation and show you how to buy the abandoned-property owner's equity with an option contract. You are really tying up the abandoned-property owner's equity with the option.

You won't exercise your option and buy the equity until you have another buyer to flip your option contract to. Remember, the abandoned-property owner was in a foreclosure situation. We will bring back just enough of the elements of your offer to buy the abandoned-property owner's equity in Chapter 9 so we can contrast this with optioning their equity.

Foreclosure Situation

Foreclosure Value	$185,000
Mortgage	−$153,000
Abandoned-Property Owner's Equity	$32,000

Your Offer

You are going to offer the abandoned-property owner $10,000 for their $32,000 equity. If you keep the property, you are going to have to pay the lender the $13,000 in back payments and foreclosure expenses to stop the foreclosure. Now you will have $23,000 in the property. If you must make repairs and do fix-up, you may have $3,000 to $5,000 more involved.

Then you add mortgage payments, property tax payments, and insurance payments. Resale costs could add another $5,000 to $10,000 or more to your investment. When you add this all up, your total is $37,000!

Your Offer

Cash to Owner	$10,000
Cash to Lender	$13,000
Repairs and Fix-Up Costs	$4,000
Carrying and Resale Costs	+$10,000
Total Invested	$37,000

Your Offer to Option the Equity

Put the same contract together with the abandoned-property owner to buy their equity. But make it an option to buy their equity. Rather than giving them $10,000 up front, give them a $1,000 option fee, which applies to the $10,000 if you exercise the option.

You now have protected your cash to the tune of $9,000. You have tied up the property. You have bought time to find another investor or buyer to flip your option to. The way we recommend you flip your option is by assigning it to the next buyer.

If you do not find a buyer to assign your option to, you have two choices. You can walk away from the deal and be out your $1,000 option fee. And the abandoned-property owner cannot sue you for specific performance.

Or you can exercise the option yourself and fix the property. Then you can sell the property to a retail buyer. Either way, by using the option you can make money through maintaining control of the property.

Making Money with an Option

Retail Buyer		Wholesale Buyer	
Sales Price	$200,000	Flip Fee	$10,000
Mortgage	−$140,000	Mortgage	−0
Gross Profit	$60,000	Gross Profit	$10,000
Invested Money	−$37,000	Invested Money	−0
Net Profit	$23,000	Net Profit	$10,000

Buyback Option

We call this use of an option having your cake and eating it too. If your first offer to the abandoned-property owner to buy their equity meets with a rejection, try using the buyback-option technique.

Normally, the buyback option is used in any situation in which someone must take the risk of sacrificing part of their equity and future appreciation in exchange for getting their hands on some immediate cash. This describes the abandoned-property owner in preforeclosure exactly.

Using a buyback option is similar to doing an equity share with the abandoned-property owner. Instead of them giving you an option, you give the abandoned-property owner an option! You present the same offer to buy their equity that they previously rejected.

Now, however, you add the feature that you will give them a buyback option if they will accept your offer. Let's put some numbers to this so you can see the beauty of the buyback option.

Using the previous example, you give the abandoned-property owner the option to buy back the property within six months for $200,000. It will be as if you fixed the property up, held on to it for six months, and sold it to a retail buyer.

Making Money with a Buyback Option

Sales Price	$200,000
Mortgage	−$140,000
Gross Profit	$60,000
Invested Money	−$37,000
Net Profit	$23,000

If you decide to flip the property to another investor for $10,000, the owner will still have the right to exercise the buyback option. The other investor will then be selling the property for a retail price minus the $10,000 they paid you.

In the next chapter, we will show you how to find motivated partners for your abandoned-property deals. Some of you have gotten to this point in the book and are excited about investing in abandoned property. You are going to put together an abandoned-property deal as soon as you come up with some investment capital. The next chapter is directed toward you.

CHAPTER 17

How to Find Motivated Partners

You may be great at finding abandoned property. You may feel confident about determining value in your target area. You are going to put together an abandoned-property deal as soon as you come up with some investment capital. This chapter is directed toward you.

We are going to show you how to use money partners to fund your abandoned-property deals. You find a great abandoned-property deal. You bring it to your money partners. They fund the deal. You split the profit with your money partners.

What Is a Partnership?

A partnership is two or more people putting together their money, brains, talents, skills, resources, and economic clout to achieve a successful investment result. A successful partnership takes more than just money. We say there are six OPs of investment partnerships. OPs stands for "other people's."

The Six OPs

The six OPs are other people's money, other people's brains, other people's talents, other people's skills, other people's resources, and other people's economic clout.

1. Other People's Money

We have found that the best money to invest is other people's money. The risk of the investment is born by the people who put up the money. If you find a super-low-risk investment with super-high returns, it is easy to find other people to fund the investment. When you help the people with the money make money, you will make money, too.

Certainly, if you have your own investment capital, you will be able to make more money doing the investment yourself. Our experience in real estate investing says the best results are obtained when you spread the risk and spread the wealth. We understand that a piece of the pie is better than no pie at all.

You could be sitting there with plenty of money to invest. Your problem is where are you going to invest it? You need to partner with someone who has the brains, skills, and talents to bring you an investment. Abandoned-property investing is your investment.

2. Other People's Brains

If you do not have the money to make an abandoned-property investment, you can have the brains to make a real estate tax lien investment. You could be one of those blessed people who have the money and the brains. However, you may still lack the talents and skills to make a successful abandoned-property investment.

If you do not feel like you have enough wattage upstairs to be comfortable making an abandoned-property investment, get a partner for your Brain Trust. In fact, if you need some help, e-mail us at thetrustee@hotmail.com. We will be glad to be your Brain Trust. By the way, the term *Brain Trust* is copywritten and trademarked.

3. Other People's Talents

Combining the talents of people to make a successful real estate investment is one of the most satisfying types of partnerships we have put together. Some people are talented at finding a good abandoned-property investment. Some people are talented at finding money partners. Some people are talented at putting together a partnership. What are your talents?

We recommend you take a blank piece of paper and start writing down what your talents are. Be bold. This is no time to be humble. You know what you are good at. This will also help you determine where you need partnership help. We know some of you are supertalented. Being the Lone Ranger doing abandoned-property investing is tough and lonely.

4. Other People's Skills

Using other people's skills can expedite your abandoned-property investing success. You need someone in your partnership who is a skilled listener. You need someone in your partnership who is a skilled negotiator. You need someone in your partnership who is a skilled leader. What are your skills?

Again, we recommend you take a blank piece of paper and start writing down what your skills are. In today's world, skills are sometimes referred to as *skill sets.*

A useful skill set for abandoned-property investing is being good with people. This means being friendly, respectful, patient, and honest. Do you have this skill set?

5. Other People's Resources

The biggest resource we have found that contributes to a successful abandoned-property investing partnership is other people's time. Time, time, time! Do you find that everything today takes too much time? (Try writing a book!) There are many details to take care of and follow up on in abandoned-property investing.

Having people in your partnership who have the time to just get things done is a godsend. Sometimes these people are called gophers. They go for this. They go for that. We have all heard the expression that time is money. This is certainly the case in any real estate investment.

6. Other People's Economic Clout

Other people's economic clout is the OPEC of real estate investing. Your goal is to have your own abandoned-property investment cartel! You don't have the cash to invest?

No problem. You don't have the economic clout to establish a credit line? No problem.

Just put someone into your partnership who has economic clout. Find someone who has the cash. Find someone who has the credit line. Find someone who has the ability to provide a strong financial statement. Remember, if you have the talent and skill to put the abandoned-property partnership cartel together, you are going to make a ton of money.

Group Investing/Syndication

Group investing is called syndication. A syndication or partnership has members of the group with matching objectives. The matching objectives in abandoned-property investing would be superhigh returns with superlow risks.

There are five main structures that are used to form a syndicate. These five structures are a corporation, a limited liability company, a general partnership, a real estate investment trust (REIT), and a limited partnership.

1. Corporation

Corporations have been around for more than one hundred years. Most big businesses are incorporated. You don't have to be a big business to incorporate.

We have two corporations. Corporations are usually formed in the state in which you are doing business. We recommend you consult with an attorney.

By forming a corporation you have central management. The main reason to form a corporation is to have limited liability. If you are doing business as a corporation and are sued, you have no personal liability. Only the corporate assets can be taken.

Of course there is a caveat. The corporate shield can be pierced by a skilled attorney. The second caveat is the double taxation of a corporation. The corporation profits are taxed at a corporate rate. The shareholders of the corporation are taxed on the dividends they receive from the corporation.

Another type of corporation is called an S corporation. This is used by people who are sole proprietors. You have the corporate liability shield. Any profits are taxed to the owner individually. There is no double taxation.

2. Limited Liability Company

An improvement on the corporation is the limited liability company. This is primarily for two or more people who want to form a partnership. They want the limited liability risk of a corporation. They do not want the double taxation and record-keeping headaches of a corporate structure.

Limited liability companies have become quite popular over the last 10 years. A limited liability company may be the ideal partnership structure for some of you to create to do abandoned-property investing. We recommend you consult with an attorney.

3. General Partnership

A general partnership is a partnership between equals. There can be two or more general partners. Each general partner has an equal say in the business of the partnership.

Unlike a corporation or a limited liability company, a general partnership has unlimited liability. Each general partner can bind the partnership. If one of the general partners is sued, all the general partners are on the hook. A general partnership must file a partnership tax return.

We feel that some type of a partnership agreement may be the simplest and easiest way to put together a group for abandoned-property investing. Again, we recommend you talk to an attorney to help you put any type of partnership agreement together.

4. Real Estate Investment Trust

A real estate investment trust, a REIT for short, is a public investment offering. Ninety percent of the net income is distributed to the shareholders. Unlike a corporation, there is no double taxation. The REIT is not taxed. Only the investors who receive distributions from the REIT are taxed.

We do not recommend REITs. They are too passive an investment for us. What we like about real estate investing is being proactive. We like being in control of our real estate investments as much as possible. This is the basis of this book and all the books in the Win Going In! series.

Some of you may be interested in a REIT that invests in abandoned property. As far as we know, no REIT makes abandoned-property investments. Check for yourself. One may come along.

5. Limited Partnership

A limited partnership can be public or private. A public limited partnership is big. A private limited partnership is small. Public limited partnerships are controlled by federal and state securities regulatory bodies.

The smallest limited partnership consists of two people. There must be one general partner. There must be one limited partner. The general partner is responsible for all decision making. The general partner chooses where and when to invest the partnership money.

The limited partner is called a limited partner because they have limited liability. The limited partner can lose no more money than the amount of money they contributed to the partnership. If a limited partner contributed $10,000 to make abandoned-property investments and the partnership lost $20,000, the limited partner could only lose their $10,000. A limited partner has no say-so in when, where, or how the partnership is going to invest.

You may want to put together money partners for abandoned-property investment purposes using a limited partnership format. You would be the general partner who would actually do all the work. The money you invested would be the partnership's money.

You would be paid a general partnership fee. After all the limited partners had their investment returned and received their profit, you may be entitled to receive additional money for your limited partnership interest.

Let's say you put together five limited partners who each contributed $100,000 to the partnership. You, as the general partner, contribute your brain, talents, and skills to make abandoned-property investments. You are paid $25,000 for your services. There is $15,000 available for expenses. This leaves $460,000 to be invested in abandoned property.

Limited Partnership

Limited Partners' Contribution	$500,000
General Partner's Fee	$25,000
Partnership Expenses	−$15,000
To Invest in Abandoned Property	$460,000

"How to Convince a Partner" Checklist

How do you convince someone to be your money partner? We are going to give you a 14-point checklist that we have found useful in our real estate investing. This checklist is not exhaustive. If you have something to add to it, then by all means do so. This is what you do at the appointment with a potential abandoned-property money partner.

1. Show Up at the Appointment on Time

This is number one on our checklist for a reason. Every one agrees that time is money. Being late to a meeting with a potential money partner sends the totally wrong signal. Why should they agree to fund your deal if you begin by not valuing their time?

2. Act Professionally

This is number two on our list for a reason. People with money want to feel comfortable with you. This is a business relationship. This is not a social relationship. A fool and their money are soon parted. Potential money partners are not fools. They have their money. Act professionally; you may get some of it.

3. Dress Accordingly

First impressions. You cannot make a first impression a second time. Business attire is appropriate for a business meeting. Dress your part. Your part is professional real estate abandoned-property investor.

4. Leave the Kids at Home

We feel this is so obvious that we almost omitted it from this checklist. You would be surprised how many business meetings we attended where the other party showed up with their children in tow. "I couldn't get a babysitter." Just doesn't make the right impression.

5. Be Honest and Friendly

People who have money can smell a rat. They will ask you questions about your knowledge and experience. Don't lie. If you have never done an abandoned-property investment and they ask you how many you have done, tell them the truth. It is all right to smile.

6. Listen, Listen, Listen

You have heard the old saying "God gave you two ears and one mouth for a reason." Find out what the money partner wants. They know you want their money.

7. *Matching, Mirroring, and Pacing*

During the conversation with the potential money partner, try matching and mirroring them. If they cross their arms, you cross your arms. If they stand up, you stand up. If they get excited, you get excited.

Pacing has to do with avoiding giving people a drink out of a fire hydrant. Yes, you want to convey your excitement about abandoned-property investing. Let the other person get excited and convey their excitement back to you.

8. *Use Your Rapport-Building Skills*

You should be good with people. If you are not, then you are the wrong person to talk to the potential money partner. Have the partner on your team who is good at building rapport with people go to the appointment.

People do business with people they like doing business with. If you are cold, distant, and arrogant, you are not going to build rapport. You are not going to get any money, either.

9. *Show Expertise and Prove It*

This is where you must have done your homework. Even if you are just starting out, you can demonstrate expertise. Have a presentation that you can make. Most people are visual. You will do far better if you have something to show the potential money partner than just winging it by flapping your lips.

10. *Compare Bank Interest Rates*

This is a follow-up to showing expertise. This is also a no-brainer. Ask the potential money partner what interest rates they are getting on their money-market accounts or certificates of deposit? They will make your case for you.

11. Compare Other Investments

Ask the potential money partner what kind of return they are getting on their stock portfolio? How well are they doing with their money-market accounts or certificates of deposit? If they are invested in real estate, ask them what they are invested in and how they are doing?

12. Be Prepared for Surprises and Have a Plan B

People who have money love to pull surprises. They may ask you to provide a name and number of someone you have worked with in abandoned-property investing. Perhaps another investor. Perhaps another money partner. They may even ask you to call them right then and there. If you tell no stories, you will not be caught in any lies.

Plan B is being able to direct the potential money partner to making an investment in something other than abandoned property. They may not be interested in abandoned property. However, they are sold on you. They may want you on their team. They may make you an offer you cannot refuse.

13. Ask for the Money

You have to ask for the money from the potential money partner. They are not going to look up and say how much money do you want? As in any business situation you must ask for the order.

We recommend you ask for the money at the beginning, middle, and end of your appointment. That way you have three chances to get a yes from your money partner.

14. Thank the Person for Their Time

Perhaps you were not successful in your quest to get a money partner. By thanking the person for their time, you leave the door open for further conversations. We have actually received a call the next day from a money partner who changed their mind.

Creative Ways to Use Partners

There is more than one way to utilize a money partner. Although they may not be willing or able to put up the money for you, here are six creative ways to use a money partner.

1. Borrow Their Financial Statement

The money partner may have no available liquid funds to invest in the partnership. The money partner may have a very strong financial statement. Give the money partner a piece of the partnership for the use of their financial statement.

You may be able to borrow money using their financial statement. In effect, you are bringing in a cosigner to create investment funds. We suggest you give the money partner the same return using their financial statement as you would if they put up the cash.

2. Borrow Their Cash

The money partner may have the cash to put in the abandoned-property partnership investment but not the inclination to do so. If abandoned-property investing is a new endeavor for them, they may not feel comfortable.

They may feel comfortable with you, however. They may loan you the money. Whether the abandoned-property investment is successful or not, you are on the hook for the return of the money partner's money.

3. Have Them Pledge Their Savings Account

The money partner may have money tied up in long-term certificates of deposit. If they cash in the certificates of deposit early, they may have to pay a substantial penalty.

Suggest they pledge the certificates of deposit for a loan or a line of credit. The certificates of deposit remain in place and act as collateral for the loan. They then have the money to invest in the partnership or loan to you for the partnership.

4. Give a Promissory Note and Pay Interest

You may have a piece of real estate that has a fairly good-size equity position. Your money partner may want the added security of a promissory note secured by the equity in your property.

Rather than just borrowing the money from the money partner and signing an unsecured note, you give them the protection of real estate. This is the same protection you have when you buy an abandoned property. The property becomes the security for your investment.

5. Use Their Line of Credit

If the money partner has a line of credit, you may be set as well. You have the line of credit set up to go. Then it is available to fund any abandoned-property purchases.

The line of credit is also useful if you are trying to make a deal with the abandoned-property owner. Cash always talks in a negotiation with the abandoned-property owner.

6. Borrow Money on Their Credit Card

You would be surprised how big a credit line some people have on their credit cards. They may also have a relatively low interest rate. You may find a money partner who would be willing to make the spread on what the partnership will pay them in interest and what the interest rate is on the cash advances on their credit card.

Partnership Agreements Checklist

In this last section, we are going to give our 21-point checklist for what must be included in any partnership agreement. We recommend you have an attorney either put together your partnership agreements or look over any partnership agreements you put together.

1. The Name of the Partnership

Although this may seem obvious to some of you, this is an important point. If you are going to get heavily involved in abandoned-property investing using partnerships, naming the partnerships becomes necessary simply from a logistics point of view.

Also, you want to take advantage of the pride factor for people in the naming of the partnership. Your money partner may want the partnership named after them. Believe it or not, this may be a deal closer for you with your money partner. Letting them name the partnership may get you the money!

2. The Term of the Partnership

All agreements must have a beginning date and an ending date. Use 36 months, and extend it if necessary. We recommend you have separate partnership agreements for each abandoned-property investment. This makes tracking your partnership investments much easier.

3. The Purpose of the Partnership

The purpose of the partnership is to make money. You want to say something such as the purpose of the partnership is to make money investing in abandoned-property real estate.

The purpose should be stated in a concise manner. Short and sweet purpose statements are best. A third party (the judge) should be able to know exactly what the purpose of the partnership is if there is a dispute between partners.

4. The Business Goals of the Partners

The business goals of the partners can be similar but also different. The business goals of the partners should be similar in the aspect of everyone wanting to make money. It doesn't work if one investor is looking for an investment loss to get a tax write-off, whereas the other investors want an investment gain.

The business goals of the partners can be different, however, with regard to acceptable rates of return on the investment. Also, some of the partners may have a longer or shorter timeline for receiving back their initial investment.

5. The Cash or Property Contributed to the Partnership

This is a very important enumeration. This is what each partner puts in to start the partnership business. It is the seed money, so to speak. Although cash is always nice, other property or resources may be necessary.

One partner may contribute office space. Another partner may contribute office equipment. Another partner may contribute their legal advice to both start the partnership and handle any legal issues down the road.

6. What Happens if More Cash Is Needed?

This is something that every partnership hopes never is going to happen. It just makes sense to have this handled in writing in the partnership agreement before there are any problems.

The partnership may need extra cash for good reasons as well as bad reasons. You may get to a tax-lien sale and find there are some deals too good to pass up. Call the money partner with the credit line and get some more partnership money invested.

7. The Skills the Partners Are Contributing

We have already talked about skills, talents, and brains as being worthwhile partnership contributions. It is important to list each partner's contributions to the partnership in these areas.

It may be especially important for you as the general partner if you may not be contributing any cash to the partnership. Down the road when the money comes in, your other partners may get greedy. Why should they give you all that money specified in the partnership agreement? Because you earned it and because of the skill sets you contributed.

8. The Distribution of the Profits

This may be the most important part of the partnership agreement. If you leave this part out in the beginning, we promise you that you will have problems in the end.

Who gets what and when is something all the partners need to know and agree on from the get-go. This way, a perfectly wonderful partnership that makes money will not be destroyed by greed and ill will.

9. What Happens if There Are Losses?

Equally important to who gets the money is who absorbs the potential losses. Although no one wants to throw a wet blanket on the excitement and enthusiasm at the beginning of the partnership, losses must be talked about.

Although it seems obvious that the partners who put up the money would absorb the losses, the losses do not have to fall on the money partners alone. It depends on how the partnership agreement decides to handle the losses. You as the general partner could agree to have your general-partnership fee reduced.

10. Salaries, Guarantees, or Drawing Accounts

Who gets paid how much, when, and for what? Who is given a guarantee? Who is authorized to take draws on the partnership bank accounts? How many partnership signatures are required on a partnership check?

The general partner typically handles the day-in, day-out business of the partnership. The general partner typically has access to the bank accounts of the partnership. The partnership may want to put in some safeguards so that the general partner, or for that matter any of the partners, cannot disappear with the partnership money.

11. Withdrawals of Contributed Assets or Capital

The partnership must decide how and when the partners can withdraw their contributed assets and capital. For example, the partner who is the attorney needs to have a cap on the amount of time they do attorney business for the partnership. Once this time is contributed, then the attorney should be compensated monetarily by the partnership for doing partnership business.

Money partners should get their initial capital back before any other partners make a profit. There is no profit to distribute until all investors are paid back their initial partnership investment. The partnership agreement must address this. Otherwise, when money comes into the partnership chaos will ensue.

12. General-Management Provisions

The partnership must have general-management provisions. This allows for the daily functioning of the partnership. Who is in charge? Who reports to whom? When must the general partner go back to the other partners for permission or guidance?

What kind of accounting procedure is going to be used? Is the partnership using accrual or cash basis? Who is going to do the accounting? Is one of the partners an accountant? Who is going to track expenses for tax purposes? Who is responsible for filing the partnership tax return?

13. Expense Accounts

Who gets to have an expense account? Who gets reimbursed for partnership expenses? When do they get reimbursed? Who reimburses them? Is the general partner in charge of tracking partnership expenses?

Expense accounts are the most easily abused partnership account. This is probably true of any business. The point is, you must treat the partnership as a business.

14. Accounting and Check-Signing Rules

All money of the partnership must be tracked. Money that comes into the partnership must be tracked. Money that goes out of the partnership, even if to other partners, must be tracked. We suggest you use ALICE.

ALICE is our acronym for assets, liabilities, income, capital, and expenses. The partnership balance sheet is made up of the partnership assets on one side and the partnership liabilities and capital on the other side. The two sides must balance. Hence the name *balance sheet.* By the way, capital is another name for net worth.

Let's say you have partnership assets of $100,000. You have partnership liabilities of $15,000. You have partnership capital or net worth of $85,000.

Balance Sheet

Assets	$100,000	Liabilities	$15,000
		Capital	$85,000
	$100,000	Totals	$100,000

The partnership profit-and-loss statement is made up of the partnership income and expenses. All the partnership income is tracked. All the partnership expenses are tracked.

When the expenses are subtracted from the income, you have a partnership profit or loss. If there is more partnership income than partnership expenses, then the partnership has a profit. If there are more partnership expenses than income, then the partnership has a loss.

15. Handling Disputes

Believe us when we tell you that every partnership will experience disputes. A dispute-resolution section in the partnership agreement must be included. We recommend voluntary arbitration first. Then we recommend binding arbitration second.

If there is still an unresolved dispute, then we recommend seeing the judge. All the partners must be aware that, once you see the judge, the partnership business is now open to public scrutiny. Keep the disputes in-house, please!

16. Sale or Assignment of a Partnership Interest

There must be a way for each partner to sell or assign their partnership interest. It is far better to allow a disgruntled partner to get out of the partnership than to force them to remain in the partnership. Establish a method to determine the value of the partnership interest in the partnership agreement.

We recommend that the other partners in the partnership have a first right of refusal to buy a departing partner's partnership interest. Again, this will be in all the partners' best interest. Who better knows the partnership than the other partners? Who better knows the value of the partnership interest than the other partners?

17. Admission of New Partners

From time to time, it may be necessary or advisable to bring in a new partner or partners to the partnership. Objective criteria must be set out in the partnership agreement as to the when and how to bring new partners aboard.

Obviously, you are looking for new partners who can bring something to the partnership. Are they bringing an infusion of cash? Are they bringing an infusion of brains, skills, or talents? In other words, why are you going to let them be partners?

18. Expulsion of a Partner

This can be a nasty and expensive undertaking. Even when the partnership agreement specifies the grounds for such an action being taken. We can't imagine how more difficult, expensive, and nasty an expulsion of a partner would be without a procedure delineated in the partnership agreement.

Our experience with expelling a partner from a partnership tells us several things. It may be in the partnership's best interest to pay the unwanted partner to go away. This may mean giving that partner more money than the partnership agreement says they are entitled to. It's your call.

19. Continuing Business if a Partner Withdraws or Dies

Unfortunately, partners sometimes get sick. Sometimes a partner gets divorced. A partner may file for bankruptcy. A partner may die. You still must be able to carry on the business of the partnership.

By covering these possibilities in the partnership agreement, you can make smoother what is never going to be a smooth transition if one of these events occurs. Remember, a partnership interest is willable. You may not want the heirs of one of your partners involved in the partnership business.

20. Determining the Value of a Departing Partner's Interest

Determining the value of a departing partner's partnership interest should be spelled out in the partnership agreement. It should really be quite cut-and-dried. If everyone agrees at the beginning of the partnership how this valuation is going to be done, then you can avoid major problems down the road.

We recommend specifying in the partnership agreement that at least one independent valuation of the partnership interest will be done. This lessens the possibility of legal action. E-mail us if you need our help.

21. Dissolution and Termination Procedures

Last but not least is a way to close down, wrap up, and put to bed the partnership. Even a successful partnership must have a way to be ended. In fact, we prefer partnerships that have a definite ending date.

Our experience with partnerships has been that when everyone knows when the partnership is going to end, it handles a basic human need for completion. If every one of the partners is happy with the results of the partnership, then close it down and start another one.

In the next chapter, we will deal with potential problems you may encounter investing in abandoned property. These potential problems include the bankruptcy of the abandoned-property owner, IRS tax liens, the destruction of the property improvements, and any environmental issues that may affect the value of the property.

CHAPTER 18

Bankruptcy and Other Problems

We will delve into four problems in this chapter. The first of these problems is an owner filing bankruptcy during your abandoned-property deal. The second problem is IRS tax liens. The third problem is the destruction of the improvements on the property before you close your abandoned-property deal. And the fourth problem is any environmental issues that may affect the value of the property and ultimately your potential profit.

Bankruptcy may delay or stop you from closing on your abandoned-property deal. An IRS tax lien can affect the title to the property you are acquiring. The destruction of the property or environmental issues may make the property you are buying worth less than the amount you are paying for the property. In fact, the environmental issues could make the property just plain worthless. Let's discuss each of these potential problems, starting with bankruptcy.

Bankruptcy

What do you do when the abandoned-property owner files for bankruptcy? If the abandoned-property owner files for bankruptcy, all of their assets are going to be frozen by the bankruptcy court. This includes any real estate holdings of the bankruptcy petitioner whether they have equity in them or not.

Bankruptcy is a legal procedure established by federal law to assist debtors that can't meet their financial obligations. The Founding Fathers of the United States were so opposed to the traditional British solution of throwing debtors into prison that they created an alternative solution.

Normally, there are two ways you will discover that the property owner has filed bankruptcy. You may be notified of the bankruptcy because you have a relationship with the owner in your abandoned-property deal. Or you may discover that the property owner has filed bankruptcy from the title insurance company when you try to record your property deed at the escrow closing.

Two Categories

Bankruptcies fall into two categories: liquidation and reorganization. In the United States, liquidation bankruptcies fall under Chapter 7 of the United States Bankruptcy Code. The debtor who takes this path ends up turning over all their nonexempt assets to the bankruptcy court. This can include their real estate holdings.

A court-appointed trustee then has the responsibility to liquidate (sell) the assets and distribute the proceeds to the existing creditors on a pro rata basis. Any debts that remain unsatisfied at that time are discharged and legally nullified. The trustee works for both the debtor and the creditors. It is the duty of the trustee to try to preserve the debtor's assets as much as possible to satisfy creditors.

Chapter 13 and Chapter 11

Bankruptcies intended to assist the debtor with financial rehabilitation through reorganization come under the categories of Chapter 13 and Chapter 11. A Chapter 13 is intended for individuals with a regular source of income. We have found that many of the owners with whom we do abandoned-property deals no longer have a regular source of income. That is why they are in financial trouble. A plan is proposed by which the debtor will continue to make payments on their debts and make up back payments with interest. A modified, extended schedule is often used to do this. This can include mortgage payments.

A Chapter 11 bankruptcy is used by corporations, partnerships, and those individuals who do not qualify for a Chapter 13 plan. The court procedures can be complex and lengthy. The cost of a Chapter 11 can be surprisingly expensive. We have found that abandoned commercial property may have owners that are corporations or partnerships that have filed a Chapter 11 bankruptcy.

New bankruptcy legislation went into effect in October 2005. The bottom line of the changes is the legislation has made it harder for people to qualify for a Chapter 7 bankruptcy wherein all of the petitioner's debts are eliminated. The emphasis now is for people to file a Chapter 13 bankruptcy and work out a repayment plan with their creditors. For this reason, the number of Chapter 7 bankruptcy filings is expected to decline significantly.

Foreclosure Stops

The moment an abandoned-property owner in foreclosure files a petition for bankruptcy, whether a Chapter 7, a Chapter 11, or a Chapter 13, any foreclosure proceedings stop immediately. This is because a legal moratorium, called an automatic stay, is imposed by the bankruptcy court. It prevents creditors from pursuing any legal actions to enforce their claims against a debtor. Said in plain English, everything *stays* put until the bankruptcy court hears the case.

If a foreclosure sale is held after a bankruptcy petition has been filed, the foreclosure will be ruled null and void by the bankruptcy judge. *Null and void* are not good words to hear from a court. From the bankruptcy court's point of view, the foreclosure sale never took place!

A mortgage lender must first seek relief from the automatic stay in order to proceed. You must do the same in order to proceed with your abandoned-property sale. The Bankruptcy Act says the court must hear a lender's petition for relief from stay within 30 days. If the court fails to do so, the stay is automatically lifted. Once the stay is lifted, the lender can proceed with their foreclosure. You can proceed with your abandoned-property sale.

Brain Trust

In a case in which you have purchased a mortgage in foreclosure from a lender and the borrower files a bankruptcy petition, you also must seek relief from the bankruptcy stay in order to proceed with your foreclosure.

Equity in Property

The amount of equity found in the property will affect the judge's decision to grant relief from the stay. If there is significant value in the property being foreclosed or sold, the judge will not grant relief from the automatic stay. The hope is that some of that equity can be used to satisfy other creditors.

If there is very little equity in the property, the judge will usually grant a relief from the automatic stay and allow the foreclosing lender to proceed. Or in the case of your abandoned-property deal, you will be able to proceed to closing.

Let's look at some examples. First we will look at a situation in which the owner has equity in the property. Then we will look at a situation in which the owner has little or no equity in the property.

An abandoned-property owner has a property worth $95,000. The property is free and clear. You make an agreement with them to buy this property for $35,000.

Equity Purchase

Owner Equity	$95,000
Your Offer	−$35,000
Equity You Pick Up	$60,000

The owner files for bankruptcy protection before you can close your abandoned-property purchase. The bankruptcy judge stays your purchase. After the judge determines there are creditors of the property owner and there is more equity in the property, the judge sets aside your purchase altogether.

The bankruptcy judge orders a bankruptcy sale of the property. The property owner has three creditors who have claims of $175,000 between them. What will happen to your abandoned-property purchase? Forget about it. It is totally gone. In fact, to add insult to injury, you are not even going to be granted creditor status for your $35,000 offer.

Highest Bidder

The highest bidder at the bankruptcy sale will receive clear title to the property. You are welcome to bid. It would be in your best interest to bid at least $35,000. That was what you were willing to pay for the property to begin with. If you want to bid more, you can.

How much more should you bid? $40,000, $50,000, $60,000? This is just like a foreclosure sale where there are lots of people bidding. You have lost the luxury of being the only buyer. Let's say you win the bid for the property with a bid of $60,000. You may still make money on the deal, but the bankruptcy filing cost you $25,000.

How will the $60,000 you paid for the property be disbursed by the bankruptcy court? The $60,000 will be allotted to the three creditors with the $175,000 in claims.

Bankruptcy Sale

Winning Bid	$60,000
Funds for Creditors	$60,000

As you can easily see, the creditors will not receive all of their claims. $60,000 to pay off $175,000 is not going to make the creditors happy. They are going to receive 40 cents on the dollar.

Creditors Receiving

Creditors Receive	$60,000
Creditors Owed	$175,000
Percentage Received	$60,000/$175,000 = 34%

No Equity in Property

What if the property owner has little or no equity in a property? This is usually the case when there is a loan on the property. Let's use the same value for the property of $95,000. This time there is a $75,000 loan on the property. Now the owner's equity position is only $20,000.

Owner's Equity

Property Value	$95,000
Loan Amount	−$75,000
Owner's Equity	$20,000

You make a deal with the owner to buy the property for $45,000. The owner's $20,000 equity position is wiped out. You then go to the lender and ask them to do a short-sale and take a $30,000 loss. (See our book *Make Money in Short-Sale Foreclosures* [John Wiley & Sons, 2006].)

Short-Sale Purchase

Loan Amount	$75,000
Your Offer	−$45,000
Lender Loss	$30,000

What happens if the owner files for bankruptcy protection before you close your short-sale because of those same three creditors who are owed $175,000? The lender is afraid of the bankruptcy court's authority to impose a court-ordered short-sale or cram down the amount of the loan payoff provision. The court may move to modify the terms of the mortgage or trust deed. This may include modifying the payment schedule to help the debtor or actually reducing the principal amount owed on the mortgage note.

The cram-down provision can only be used with reorganization types of bankruptcies (Chapters 11 and 13) in which the property plays a key role in the reorganization plan. In other words, the debtor must have a substantial equity position in the property and have a reliable source of income to qualify for a reorganization plan.

Neither of these conditions applied in this case. The owner had very little equity in the property and no reliable source of income. We petitioned the court to remove the automatic stay so that we could proceed with our short-sale. The bankruptcy judge lifted the stay for our deal.

There was no money in the property for the creditors to receive funds. The lender was already being crammed down by our short-sale offer. In fact, by the owner filing the bankruptcy, the lender was practically forced to accept our short-sale offer. Otherwise the judge could have forced them to get even less in the deal.

Our experience with abandoned-property owners filing for bankruptcy has been positive. It just may take a little more time to close your abandoned-property deal when a bankruptcy occurs. Bankruptcy is not necessarily an abandoned-property deal killer. We are going to complete our discussion about bankruptcy by mentioning a few twists especially around the foreclosure arena.

Creative Debtors

Debtors have come up with some pretty creative ways to stall foreclosures. Maybe you thought that a person only can file a bankruptcy once every seven years. That is true of Chapter 7 liquidations but not true with Chapters 11 and 13 reorganizations.

The law does not prohibit the act of filing bankruptcy, and it is the filing that brings on the automatic stay. Because of this, a growing number of debtors are using that loophole to further delay the foreclosure process. Many judges are now wise to this trickery and will quickly lift the new stay.

Bankruptcies Filed after a Foreclosure Sale

Cases have been reported in which a bankruptcy judge has overturned a foreclosure sale that occurred just prior to the filing of the bankruptcy petition. The judge may rule that the equity in the property could have been used to pay more creditors.

Because the Bankruptcy Code is a federal law, a debtor in any state can file a bankruptcy petition and stop the foreclosure process. If the bankruptcy petition is filed 15 days into the foreclosure, the foreclosure will resume on the 15th day after the automatic stay is lifted. In other words, the lender does not have to go back to the beginning of the foreclosure. They resume the foreclosure from its current point. Now let's see what happens if there is an IRS tax lien on the property.

IRS Tax Liens

What happens to your abandoned-property deal if there is an IRS tax lien recorded against the abandoned-property owner's property? The IRS tax lien can be a junior or senior lien in relationship to other liens against the property. A lien is junior or senior to another lien based on the priority of when the lien was recorded. Earlier recording gives one lien seniority over another lien. The dollar amount of the lien does not determine its seniority.

The IRS tax lien can cloud the title to the property. You may find it difficult to get marketable title to the property while the tax lien is still in place. From our discussion of the elements of value, which included transferability, you may find the property difficult to resell. Sometimes you or your buyer can negotiate with the IRS to pay part of the lien to get it off the property. This is buying the tax lien for less than its face amount.

Foreclosure

If the IRS lien is senior to the lien of a foreclosing lender, the buyer at the foreclosure sale takes title to the property subject to the existing IRS tax lien. If you are doing a short-sale with this lender, you also would take title to the property subject to the IRS lien.

If the tax lien is junior to the foreclosing lender, the IRS must be notified and has the right to sell the property again within 120 days of the foreclosure sale. The IRS will do this if they think there is more equity in the property to get money to pay the tax lien. The IRS must pay back the investor who bought the property at the foreclosure sale their purchase money and expenses.

Short-Sale

This can affect your short-sale with a lender who is in a senior position to an IRS lien. It is smart not to do any improvements or fix up the property until the 120 days has expired. If you do and IRS sells the property, you might want to be the new buyer to protect your investment! Of course, you may then wind up overpaying for the property. Now let's turn our attention to what happens to your abandoned-property deal when the improvements on the property are destroyed before you close your deal.

Destruction of Improvements

Though this is a fairly unlikely occurrence, it is possible. A fire, hurricane, tornado, or natural disaster could destroy the home or the improvements on the property. In 2003 we came very close to buying two properties on the Gulf Coast in Mississippi. The first was a six-story historic hotel in Biloxi. The second was an antebellum home in Pass Christian. Both were destroyed by Hurricane Katrina in 2005. Sometimes the best deals you make are the ones you don't make!

This may not be as bad as it sounds. Most property owners carry casualty insurance. This will cover the cost of repairs. In some cases, the casualty insurance will pay off the outstanding liens if there is a total loss.

We have discovered, however, that many abandoned-property owners have let their casualty insurance lapse after they have abandoned the property. So you may want to consider taking out an insurance binder during the escrow or closing period to protect your investment.

Value of the Land

Sometimes the value of the land is greater than the value of the improvements on the land. Then, even if the improvements on the property are destroyed, the property retains sufficient value for you to have enough security to continue with your abandoned-property deal.

For some of you, this may be a research consideration. You may want to make sure that the land is worth more than the buildings. You can get a sense of the value of the land and the value of the improvements by looking at the allocation between the land and the improvements given by the local property-taxing authority. This can be found on the property-tax bill for the property. Finally we will discuss environmental issues that can affect your abandoned-property deal.

Environmental Issues

This is a fairly rare occurrence. Your initial research will usually turn up any existing environmental issues. If there is an environmental problem in the area, keep away from buying abandoned property in that area. Do not buy abandoned residential property near commercial property that could be contaminated.

There could be a problem with contamination if the site was formerly an auto repair shop, a dry cleaner, a gas station, a chemical plant, a printing business, or a paint factory. Environmental issues are one of the reasons we recommended you particularly scrutinize commercial properties.

In a normal purchase situation, you may be able to require the property owner to mitigate any adverse environmental issues before the closing. In an abandoned-property deal, the property owner may not have the financial wherewithal to do anything about these adverse environmental issues.

These environmental issues will become your problem once you become the owner of the property. Once you discover environmental issues, we recommend you back out of the abandoned-property deal. Can you spell EPA?

Foreclosing Decision

If you buy the mortgage in foreclosure and wind up foreclosing and taking title to the property, you may be in for a big surprise. If the property is contaminated by toxic waste, hazardous chemicals, mold, radon gas, or lead paint, you may be liable for the cleanup costs as the property owner.

Of course, this would be the case only if you foreclosed on your mortgage and acquired the deed to the property. No one says you have to foreclose on your mortgage. You could wait it out and see if the property is eventually cleaned up. Your mortgage is still a lien against the title to the property. Eventually, your mortgage may be paid off.

Other than doing your homework, there is not much more that you can do to avoid environmental problems. The best way to protect yourself from losing your personal assets to pay for environmental cleanup is to never own property in your name.

We suggest protecting yourself by incorporating your abandoned-property investment business. Incorporation provides a shield for your personal assets. The most you will lose is the amount you have in the corporation's name.

You could also form a limited liability company (an LLC). You could be a limited partner in a limited partnership. All of these structures provide you with personal asset protection.

The likelihood that any of the four problems we have discussed in this chapter will happen is relatively small. The abandoned-property owner filing bankruptcy is the most likely occurrence statistically. An IRS tax lien is the second most likely occurrence. The destruction of the property improvements is less likely. An environmental problem is the least likely occurrence statistically.

In the next chapter, we will give you important information about escrow, closing, and title insurance that you need to complete your successful abandoned-property deal. We will give you a warning right now. Never buy real estate without obtaining title insurance!

CHAPTER 19

Closing Your Abandoned-Property Deal

In this chapter we will discuss the paperwork of real estate, escrow, closing, and title insurance. This has to do with you actually receiving the title to the property at the conclusion of your abandoned-property deal. Without the transfer of ownership from the property owner to you, there may not be much profit for you in the deal. A transfer of ownership revolves around escrow, closing, and title insurance.

Real Estate Paperwork

Understanding the paperwork of real estate is critical to your success as an abandoned-property real estate investor. We are going to talk about the paperwork involved in ownership title and lender financing.

There are three aspects to the title and lending paperwork. First, there is the paperwork involved on the title side. Second, there is the paperwork involved on the financing side. Finally, there is the paperwork that bridges the title and financing sides and is known as the security side.

Title Side

On the title side, there are two types of deeds used through-out the country to convey the property title from one owner to the next. These deeds are grant deeds and warranty deeds. To find out which deed is used in your state, check with a real estate broker or your local title insurance company.

Grant Deed

A grant deed is a deed using the word *grant* in the clause that awards ownership. This written document is used by the grantor (seller) to transfer the title of their property to the grantee (buyer). Grant deeds have two implied warranties. One is that the grantor has not previously transferred the title. The other is that the title is free from encumbrances that are not visible to the grantee. This deed also transfers title acquired after delivery of the deed from the seller to the buyer.

Warranty Deed

A warranty deed is a deed in which the grantor (usually the seller) guarantees the title to the property to be in the condition indicated in the deed. The grantor agrees to protect the grantee (usually the buyer) against all claims to the property made by anyone other than holders of recorded liens (matters of record). A warranty deed gives a warranty to the title holder.

Grant Deed		Warranty Deed	
Grantor	Grantee	Grantor	Grantee
(Seller or Owner)	(Buyer)	(Seller or Owner)	(Buyer)

Financing Side

The paperwork involved on the financing side is the evidence of the debt. The two types of paperwork that are used as evidence of the debt are the promissory note and the mortgage note. This paperwork is used by lenders and borrowers to create a written agreement about the terms and conditions for the real estate loan.

Promissory Note

A *promissory note* is the written contract a borrower signs promising to pay back a definite amount of money to a lender by a definite future date. A promissory note has four basic elements. These are the amount of the note, the interest rate of the note, the term of the note, and the payments, if any, on the note. A promissory note that has no payments till the due date of the note is called a straight note.

Mortgage Note

A mortgage note is a written contract signed by a borrower in which the borrower agrees to pay back a lender the amount of money the lender loaned the borrower. Similar to a promissory note, a mortgage note specifies the amount of the note, the interest rate of the note, the term of the note, and the payments on the note.

Promissory Note		**Mortgage Note**	
Borrower (Maker of the Note)	Lender (Holder of the Note)	Borrower (Maker of the Note)	Lender (Holder of the Note)

Security Side

The paperwork involved on the security side is trust deeds and mortgages. They are regarded as security devices for the promissory notes and mortgage notes, respectively. Another way to say this is the trust deeds and mortgages are the collateral for the lender in the event a borrower defaults on the loan.

They become liens against the property title when they are officially recorded at the county recorder's office in the county where the property that is the security or collateral for the lien is located. To find out which security device is used in your state, check with a real estate broker or your local mortgage lender.

Trust Deed

A trust deed is a document used as a security device for a loan on a property by which the owner transfers bare (naked) legal title with the power of sale to a trustee. This transfer is in effect until the owner totally pays off the loan.

There are three parties to a trust deed. These three parties are the trustor, the trustee, and the beneficiary. The trustor is the owner/borrower who transfers the bare legal title with a power of sale to the trustee. The trustee is a person who holds the bare legal title to a property without being the actual owner of the property. The trustee has the power of sale for the lender's benefit. The beneficiary is the lender of money on a property used in a trust deed type of loan.

Trust Deed

1. Trustor	2. Trustee	3. Beneficiary
(Borrower)	(Power of Sale)	(Lender)

Mortgage Contract

A mortgage contract is a document used as a security device for a loan on a property by which the owner/borrower promises their property as security or collateral without giving up possession of or title to the property.

There are two parties to a mortgage contract. These two parties are the mortgagor and the mortgagee. The mortgagor is the owner/borrower who uses a mortgage contract to borrow money. The mortgagee is the lender of money on a property used in a mortgage contract type of loan.

Mortgage Contract

1. Mortgagor	2. Mortgagee
(Borrower)	(Lender)

What It All Means

Foreclosure is possible because of the paperwork of real estate. The relationship of the title paperwork, the financing paperwork, and the security paperwork gives the lender the ability to protect themselves when they loan money to a borrower.

The security paperwork—trust deeds and mortgages—is the bridge between the ownership, or title, side and the finance side. The promissory notes and mortgage notes create the security devices that become liens against the title to the property.

Once you understand the paperwork of real estate, you will be able to negotiate on an equal footing with lenders. All this paperwork comes down to contracts. All contracts come down to what the paperwork says. When you understand what the paperwork says, then you can control what happens to property. See if this next illustration helps clarify the paperwork relationships.

The Paperwork

Title	Security Devices (The Bridge)	Finance
Grant Deed or Warranty Deed	Trust Deed————————Promissory Note	
	Trustor/Trustee	
Grantor/ Grantee	Beneficiary	
(Seller)/ (Buyer)	(Lender)	
	Mortgage————————Mortgage Note	
	Mortgagor/Mortgagee	
	(Borrower)/(Lender)	

Escrow

Escrow is a type of closing by which you and the property owner deposit money and/or documents with a neutral third party, the escrow holder. Whoever handles the closing of your abandoned property's transaction acts as an agent for you and the property owner. You and the property owner give the escrow holder instructions to hold and disburse documents and funds after certain conditions are met. The escrow holder acts as an impartial stakeholder and communicates with everyone involved in the transaction.

We recommend having an escrow because of the complexity of the closing process. The advantages of escrow are that the escrow holder is responsible for keeping documents and funds safe; making computations; receiving and distributing funds; carrying out the terms of the real estate contract; complying with federal, state, and local tax regulations; providing an accounting for the transfer process; and determining that all conditions have been satisfied.

An escrow is complete when all conditions listed in the escrow instructions are met and all acts specified in the instructions are performed. When an escrow is complete, the escrow holder disburses the funds and documents to close the escrow.

In its simplest format, an escrow would have the buyer put the money in the escrow account at the opening of the escrow. The seller would take the money out of the escrow at the closing of the escrow. The seller would put the deed to the property in escrow at the opening of the escrow. The buyer would take the deed to the property out of the escrow at the closing of the escrow.

Many things are occurring during the escrow period: termite inspections, physical inspections, money-partner inspections, geological inspections, title searches, procuring hazard insurance, obtaining financing, preparing loan documents, calculating closing costs, preparing deeds, and so on.

Escrow holders are usually prohibited from offering advice, negotiating with you and the property owner, revealing information about the escrow to people who are not a party to the escrow, and preparing or revising escrow instructions without the authorization of you and the property owner. So how do you open an escrow?

Opening an Escrow

Consider choosing an escrow holder who is willing to take the time to explain what is happening and what you need to do. Choose a company that is located a convenient distance from where you live so you can deliver and sign documents or deliver money easily.

Depending on your area, the party that acts as the escrow holder may include independent escrow companies, escrow departments of lending institutions, title insurance companies, real estate brokers, and real estate attorneys. You may find that your area does a closing with an attorney rather than conducting an escrow.

After you select an escrow holder, open the escrow by following these steps:

1. Contact the escrow holder by telephone or in person. (We don't recommend your initial contact be by e-mail.)
2. Give the escrow holder all the relevant information regarding the sale.
3. Deposit the earnest money with the escrow holder, preferably in person or, if necessary, by certified mail.

The escrow officer collects the information necessary to prepare escrow instructions on a form called a *take sheet*. Data the escrow holder may need to prepare escrow instructions include the following:

1. Property description.
2. Parties to the transaction.
3. Proposed closing date.
4. Sales price.
5. Loans currently on the property. (This is important in a short-sale.)
6. Loans buyer wants to put on the property.
7. Vesting of the title in the new owner.
8. Conditions of the title, such as the conditions, covenants, and restrictions.
9. Buyer's and seller's costs.

So what are escrow instructions about?

Escrow Instructions

Escrow instructions are the written agreement between you and the property owner that translates the real estate contract into a form used by the escrow holder to conduct and close the escrow. The escrow holder prepares the escrow instructions, using the take sheet as a guideline, so that the intent and conditions are identical to those in the contract. The escrow holder then asks you and the owner to read and sign the escrow instructions.

You should read the escrow instructions carefully. Make sure that the intent and conditions of the escrow instructions are identical to those in the purchase contract. Ask questions about items you do not understand or ones that do not appear to match those in the contract. Sign the escrow instructions only when you are satisfied that all items reflect exactly the terms of the purchase contract.

You and the property owner can make amendments (changes) to the escrow instructions. To do so, discuss the changes with the owner and obtain their agreement to make the change. Request that the escrow holder prepare documents for the change and send these documents to you and the owner. Sign the documents authorizing the change (the owner must also sign) and return the documents to the escrow holder. Now you are ready to close.

Closing

Understanding how the escrow closes can make you comfortable with a process many buyers and sellers find very confusing. Closing is the process in which funds and property title are transferred between you and the abandoned-property owner. Although closing could be accomplished by you and the property owner simply getting together and exchanging money and documents, most real estate transactions today use an escrow type of closing. So how are prorations handled?

The Buyer's Day

The day the escrow closes is considered the buyer's day. What this means is that all the prorations of property taxes, hazard insurance, mortgage interest, and property rents are figured on this day. Prorations are the apportionment of charges owed on the property between the seller and the buyer.

Let's say the escrow closes on the 14th day of the month. The seller is responsible for paying the property taxes, hazard insurance, and mortgage interest through the 13th day of the month. If the property is receiving rental income, the seller is entitled to receive a prorated share of the monthly rent through the 13th day of the month. This is because rents are paid in advance, usually on the first day of the month.

The buyer is responsible for paying the property taxes, hazard insurance, and mortgage interest starting on the 14th day of the month. If the property is receiving rental income, the buyer is entitled to receive a prorated share of the monthly rent from the 14th day of the month until the end of the month.

Quick-Cash Caveat

Using our quick-cash system, you may wind up receiving money directly from another real estate investor without going to a closing. You could be flipping a property before the closing. You could be assigning a purchase contract or an option contract to another investor, who will then go to a closing with a seller rather than you.

Closing Statement

Once the escrow closes, a closing statement is prepared by the escrow holder. In the United States, all closing statements are referred to as a HUD 1. HUD stands for the Department of Housing and Urban Development. We have our escrow holder prepare an estimated HUD 1 to submit with our short-sale offer to the lender. That way, the lender can see how much money they will receive at the closing as a result of accepting our short-sale offer.

The closing statement is set up as a debit and credit accounting. The purchase price appears as a credit to the seller and a debit to the buyer. Any rental security deposits will be credited to the buyer and debited to the seller. Everything else will be prorated as a debit and a credit to the seller and buyer, respectively, based on the day of closing. Let's talk about title insurance next.

Title Insurance

We have talked about the four elements of value. They are demand, utility, scarcity, and transferability. We feel the most important element of value for you to consider when you invest in abandoned property is transferability.

Transferability refers to the ease and seamlessness involved in transferring the title or ownership interest in a property from the current owner to a new owner. If there is an ease and seamlessness in transferring title, the value of the property goes up. This is true for both the current owner and the new owner. If there are difficulty and problems in transferring title, the value of the property goes down. Again, this is true for both the current owner and the new owner.

If you buy abandoned property, get title insurance. *Never buy abandoned property without title insurance.* What is title insurance? Title insurance is a policy of insurance issued to you by a title company on completion of the final title search, which protects your title to property against claims made in the future based on circumstances in the past.

Title insurance is especially important when you are investing in abandoned properties. Liens and encumbrances against the property title tend to mushroom with abandoned properties. There may be tax liens, lawsuits, and other creditors with interests against the title to the property.

There are exceptions to our rule regarding buying title insurance. We know of an investor who bids on foreclosure properties on the courthouse steps and does no preliminary research on either the condition of the title or the property. If he wins a bid, he goes inside the courthouse and checks the condition of the title using the public records. At the same time, he has a partner do a drive-by inspection of the property.

He takes advantage of the two-hour window the foreclosing trustee allows for the winning bidder to produce the cash or cashier's checks. If the property looks like a bomb (not *the bomb*), he backs out of the deal. If he discovers problems too great for him to handle with the title to the property, he backs out of the deal. This is found out through a title search.

Title Search

A title search is an examination of information recorded on a property, or the owner of the property, at the county recorder's office in the county where the property is located. The examination verifies that the property will have no outstanding liens or claims against it to adversely affect a buyer or lender when the title to the property is transferred to a new buyer or pledged as collateral for a real estate loan.

When you are buying property, especially an abandoned property, it is always a good idea to get a preliminary title report from a title insurance company. The preliminary title report is usually produced by the title company during the escrow or closing. The purpose of the preliminary report is to make everyone—buyer, seller, lender, escrow holder, title company—aware of the condition of the title involved in the transaction. Let's talk about the types of title policies: the owner's, buyer's, and lender's policies.

Owner's Policy

An owner's policy of title insurance protects the owner of record from claims against the title brought by other parties. If a claim arises and you have title insurance, and any monetary damages are to be paid, the title insurance company will pay them. By the way, the seller or buyer can pay for the owner's policy. You want to get the owner's policy of title insurance on all your short-sale deals. This will protect your great short-sale investment from potential disaster.

Buyer's Policy

A buyer's policy of title insurance protects the buyer of real estate. The buyer's policy is similar to the lender's policy in that it protects the buyer for matters beyond what is in the public record. Although the buyer becomes the owner and is protected by the owner's policy, a buyer may feel they want extended coverage. We recommend getting buyer's coverage any time you are involved in a foreclosure transaction.

Lender's Policy

A lender's policy of title insurance protects the real estate lender beyond matters of public record. There may be unrecorded liens against the title. A lender wants to be protected against everything because they have so much money loaned on the property. Typically, the lender makes the buyer who is using the loan proceeds to complete the purchase of the property pay for the lender's title policy.

Abandoned-Property Closings

We recommend you find an escrow holder who is adept at handling abandoned-property closings. It becomes very important if you are using the same escrow holder to handle the buying portion of the abandoned-property transaction and the simultaneous selling portion of the abandoned-property transaction.

An escrow holder who has a strong relationship with a title insurance company is your best bet. The key is making sure you receive clear title. A good escrow company or closing attorney will make sure all the i's are dotted and all the t's are crossed as they coordinate the closings with the title insurance company.

CONCLUSION

Congratulations on completing *Make Money in Abandoned Properties.* We know you have a lot of material to digest. Our hope is that we have stimulated your interest in making money with abandoned properties.

Our recommendation is for you to go back to the areas that are of the most interest for you. Reread them, and then get started. Look at property. Schedule an appointment with an owner of an abandoned property. Write an offer! Present the offer! Our point is, do something! Make some money.

We are always coming up with more creative possibilities for investments and problem solving. So, as we bid you adieu, we have this to say to you: Get creative! Pull a group of people together and contact us for a seminar.

Are you a Lone Ranger right now? You won't be for long when you start making money in abandoned properties. Meanwhile, you can e-mail us for fee-based consulting. We are always open to new possibilities, so let us know if you need a partner. Get out there and do something *now!*

Let us know what did or didn't work for you. We want to hear about your experiences in the abandoned-property arena. You can contact us through our publisher, e-mail us at thetrustee@hotmail.com, or write to us at P.O. Box 274, Bedford, Texas 76095-0274.

Remember to watch for more of this Win Going In! series. The first book in the series was *The New Path to Real Estate Wealth: Earning Without Owning.* The second was

Quick Cash in Foreclosures. The third book was *Make Money in Real Estate Tax Liens: How to Guarantee Returns Up to 50%.* The fourth book was *Make Money in Short-Sale Foreclosures,* and this book is the fifth. Watch for further topics in this Win Going In! series. God bless y'all!

—*Chantal & Bill Carey*

A PPENDIX A

Deeds Chart

For use in the United States. All other areas please check with
your local law agent.

G = Grant deed is a deed using the word grant in the clause
that awards ownership. This written document is used by
the grantor (seller) to transfer title to the grantee (buyer).
Grant deeds have two implied warranties. One is that the
grantor has not previously transferred the title. The other
is that the title is free from encumbrances that are not
visible to the grantee. This deed also transfers any title
acquired by the grantor after delivery of the deed.

W = Warranty deed is a deed in which the grantor (usually
the seller) guarantees the title to be in the condition
indicated in the deed. The grantor agrees to protect the
grantee (usually the buyer) against all claimants to the
property.

* = Special deed.

STATE	DEEDS	STATE	DEEDS
Alabama	W	Delaware	G
Alaska	W	Washington, D.C.	G
Arizona	G	Florida	W
Arkansas	G	Georgia	W
California	G	Hawaii	W
Colorado	W	Idaho	W
Connecticut	W	Illinois	G,W

(continued)

STATE	DEEDS	STATE	DEEDS
Indiana	W	North Carolina	W
Iowa	W	North Dakota	G,W
Kansas	W	Ohio	W
Kentucky	W	Oklahoma	G
Louisiana	W	Oregon	W
Maine	W	Pennsylvania	G
Maryland	W	Puerto Rico	*
Massachusetts	W	Rhode Island	W
Michigan	W	South Carolina	G,W
Minnesota	W	South Dakota	W
Mississippi	W	Tennessee	W
Missouri	W	Texas	G
Montana	G	Utah	W
Nebraska	W	Vermont	W
Nevada	G	Virginia	G
New Hampshire	W	Washington	W
New Jersey	G,W	West Virginia	G
New Mexico	W	Wisconsin	W
New York	G	Wyoming	W

A PPENDIX B

Loans Chart

For use in the United States. All other areas please check with your local law agent.

M = Mortgage, a contract by which you promise your property without giving up possession of the property to secure a loan. You also retain title to the property.

TD = Trust deed, a contract used as a security device for a loan on your property, by which you transfer bare (naked) legal title with the power of sale to a trustee. This transfer is in effect until you have totally paid off the loan. In the meantime you have possession of the property.

* = Mortgage preferred; trust deed also valid.

** = Trust deed preferred; mortgage also valid.

*** = Use note to secure debt.

STATE	DEEDS	STATE	DEEDS
Alabama	M,TD	Florida	M,TD
Alaska	M,TD	Georgia	***
Arizona	M,TD	Hawaii	M
Arkansas	M	Idaho	M,TD
California	TD	Illinois	M,TD
Colorado	TD	Indiana	M,TD
Connecticut	M	Iowa	M,TD
Delaware	M	Kansas	M
Washington, D.C.	TD	Kentucky	M,TD*

(*continued*)

STATE	DEEDS	STATE	DEEDS
Louisiana	M	Ohio	M
Maine	M	Oklahoma	M,TD
Maryland	M,TD	Oregon	M,TD
Massachusetts	M	Pennsylvania	M
Michigan	M	Puerto Rico	M
Minnesota	M	Rhode Island	M
Mississippi	M,TD**	South Carolina	M,TD
Missouri	TD	South Dakota	M
Montana	M,TD*	Tennessee	TD
Nebraska	M,TD	Texas	TD
Nevada	M,TD	Utah	M,TD
New Hampshire	M	Vermont	M
New Jersey	M	Virginia	M,TD*
New Mexico	M,TD	Washington	M,TD
New York	M	West Virginia	TD
North Carolina	M,TD	Wisconsin	M
North Dakota	M,TD	Wyoming	M,TD

GLOSSARY

Abatement notice A notice to decrease or cease an illegal or unreasonable irritant that hurts, hinders, or damages others or creates a repeated or persisting interference with another's right.

Abstract of title A summary of the history of ownership of a property from public records. This history includes all changes of ownership and claims against the property.

Acceleration clause A provision in a loan document that makes the balance owed on a loan due and payable immediately after a specified event occurs. The event may be missing a payment or violating another provision of the loan.

Acknowledgment A formal declaration before a public official that one has signed a specific document.

Adjustable rate loan Adjustable rate mortgage, ARM; a loan that al-lows adjustments in the interest rate at specified times based on a named index.

Adjustable rate mortgage See Adjustable rate loan.

Adjusted basis The original cost plus capital improvements minus depreciation. Use adjusted basis to compute taxable gain or loss on the sale of a home.

Adjusted sales price As a seller, the price for which you sell your home minus closing costs and commission, if applicable.

Agent A person authorized by another, the principal, to act for him or her in dealing with third parties.

AITD See All-inclusive trust deed.

Alienation clause See Due-on-sale clause.

All-inclusive trust deed AITD, Wraparound mortgage; a junior (sec-ond, third, and so forth) loan (mortgage or trust deed) at one overall interest rate used to wrap the existing loans into a package. The amount is sufficient to cover the existing loans and provide additional funds for the sellers. Sellers pay on existing loans from buyers' payments. Sellers remain primarily responsible for the original loans.

Amortization Gradual paying off of the principal on a loan by payment of regular installments of principal and interest.

Annual percentage rate APR; an interest rate that includes interest, discount points, origination fees, and loan broker's commission.

Appraisal An examination of a property by a qualified professional to estimate the property's market value as of a specific date.

APR See Annual percentage rate.

Arbitration Taking of a controversy to an unbiased third person. This person holds a hearing at which both parties may speak and then issues an opinion.

ARM See Adjustable rate loan.

Assessment Tax or charge by a governmental body for a specific public improvement covering the property owner's portion of costs. Assessments are in addition to normal property taxes.

Assign Transfer.

Assignee The person to whom interest is transferred.

Assignment Transfer of any property to another. Delegation of duties and rights to another.

Assignor The person from whom interest is transferred.

Assume Buyers taking over primary responsibility for payment of existing loan. Sellers then become secondarily liable for the loan and for any deficiency judgment.

Assumption fee Transfer fee; the fee a lender may charge for work involved in allowing buyers to assume primary liability for payment on an existing loan.

Attorney A person licensed to practice law by giving legal advice or assistance, as well as prosecuting and defending cases in courts.

Authorization to sell   A listing contract allowing a real estate professional to act as an agent in the sale of property. (See also Listing.)

Bankruptcy   Relief by a court of an obligation to pay money owed after turning over all property to a court-appointed trustee.

Basis   The cost of a home when purchased, including down payment, loans, and closing costs.

Beneficiary   The lender of money on a property used in a trust deed type of loan.

Beneficiary statement   A statement provided by a lender using a trust deed type of loan that usually lists claims that do not appear on loan documents.

Bill of lading   A contract for the transportation of your goods with a commercial moving company.

Binder   An informal contract listing an agreement's main points, later replaced by a formal, detailed written contract.

Breach of contract   Failure to perform as promised without a legal excuse (a good reason).

Bridge loan   A short-term loan to buyers who are simultaneously selling one house and trying to buy another.

Broker   See Real estate broker.

Building codes   Regulations by governments giving requirements and standards for structures built in their jurisdictions.

Building permits   County-issued documents that permit you to build after your plans have been approved by the necessary city and county agencies.

Buyer's agent   Selling agent; a real estate broker or sales associate who represents the buyer in a transaction.

Buyer's broker   A real estate broker who represents the buyer. (See also Real estate broker.)

Buyer's fees   Charges that are paid for by the buyers.

Buyer's market   A condition in which there are more sellers than buyers; prices generally decrease.

Call   Demand payment of a debt.

Capital asset   Property, both real and personal, held by a taxpayer and not excluded by tax laws.

Capital gain   Profit from selling or exchanging a capital asset in excess of the cost.

Capital improvements   Additions to property that are permanent, increase property value, and have a useful life of more than one year.

Capitalization rate   The rate of return an investment receives.

Capital loss   Loss from selling or exchanging property other than a personal residence at less than its cost.

Cashier's check   A bank's own check guaranteed to be good by the bank at which it is drawn.

Casualty   Loss of or damage to structures or personal property.

Casualty insurance   See Hazard insurance.

CC&Rs   Covenants, conditions, and restrictions; a document listing private restrictions on property. Often used when buyers have an interest in common areas.

Certificate of title   A report, produced by a party providing abstracts of titles, stating that based on an examination of public records, the title is properly vested in the present owner.

Classified advertisements   Advertisements that are separated by type and listed accordingly.

Closing   Closing escrow, settlement; the final phase of a real estate transaction that involves signing loan documents, paying closing costs, and delivering the deed. (See also Escrow.)

Closing costs   Costs of sale; the additional expenses over and above the purchase price of buying and selling real estate.

Closing escrow   See Closing.

Closing fee   See Closing costs.

Closing statement   A written, itemized account given to both sellers and buyers at closing by the escrow holder and detailing receipts, disbursements, charges, credits, and prorations.

Commission   Payments to an agent, such as a real estate broker, for services in the selling or buying of a home.

Commitment   An oral or written agreement to make a loan made by a lender to a potential buyer.

Competent person   A person who meets certain criteria set by a state for competency. These laws often include being a natural person who is an adult or an emancipated minor, mentally competent, and not a felon deprived of civil rights; an artificial person may also meet the requirements.

Completion bond   A bond ensuring that if a contractor does not complete a project, an insurance company will pay for the remaining work to be done.

Completion notice   Copy of the document you file and record with your county when work on your home is complete; it places time limits for mechanics' liens.

Condemnation   The act of taking private property for public use after payment of a fair price (compensation).

Conditions   Requirements that must precede the performance or effectiveness of something else. Provisions or qualifications in a deed that if violated or not performed nullify the deed.

Condominium   An undivided ownership in common in a portion of a piece of real property plus a separate interest in space in a building.

Consideration   Anything of value that influences a person to enter into a contract including money, a deed, an item of personal property, an act (including the payment of money), a service, or a promise (such as to pay on a loan). Acts or services must be performed after you and the buyers enter into the contract.

Contingency   A condition on which a valid contract depends.

Contingency release   Wipeout clause, kick-out provision; provisions providing that you will continue to market your home until you receive another offer to purchase your home that does not contain the contingencies you indicated or buyers remove those contingencies you specified. After you receive a contract without the detailed contingencies, the original buyers have the specified time you agreed on to remove the contingencies or you may sell your home to the buyers who offered you a contract without the contingencies.

Contract for deed   See Land sales contract.

Controller's deed   See Tax deed.

Conventional loan   A loan that is not guaranteed or insured by a government agency.

Convey   Transfer.

Costs of sale   See Closing costs.

Counteroffer   A statement by a person to whom an offer is made proposing a new offer to the original offeror.

Counterparts   Two documents considered as one.

Covenants   Agreements or promises contained in and conveyed by a deed that are inseparable from the property; pledges for the performance or nonperformance of certain acts or the use or nonuse of property.

Cram-down provision   See Short-sale provision.

Credit report   A detailed report of a person's credit history and rating.

Dedication   A giving of land by a property owner to the public for public use.

Deed   A document containing a detailed written description of the property that transfers property ownership.

Deed of trust   See Trust deed.

Default   Failure of a person to fulfill an obligation or perform a duty; failure to make a loan payment when it is due.

Default insurance   See Mortgage default insurance.

Deficiency judgment   A court decision making an individual personally liable for payoff of a remaining amount due because the full amount was not obtained by foreclosure.

Delinquent payment   A payment that was not paid when it was due.

Demand fee   Demand for payoff charge; a fee for a written request to a lender for lender's demand for payment of the loan in full and the supporting documents necessary for release of the lien against the property.

Demand for payoff charge   See Demand fee.

Deposit   Money that buyers submit with a purchase offer as evidence of their intention and ability to buy.

Depreciation   Loss in value from any cause.

Disclosure   Making known things that were previously unknown.

Discount points   See Points.

Discovery   Disclosure of things previously unknown.

Discrimination   Giving or withholding particular advantages to or from certain types of persons arbitrarily selected from a larger group. Treating other persons unfairly or denying them normal privileges.

Display advertisements   Large advertisements that often contain illustrations.

Divided agency   Agent's action in representing both parties in a transaction without the knowledge and consent of both.

Documentary transfer tax   See Transfer tax.

Down payment   Money that you and buyers agree on, or that a lender requires, that buyers pay toward the purchase price before escrow can close.

Drawing deed fee   A fee for the preparation of a deed.

Dual agent   A broker acting either directly, or through an associate licensee, as agent for both seller and buyer.

Due-on-sale clause   Alienation clause; an acceleration clause in a loan giving the lender the right to demand all sums owed due at once and payable if the property owner transfers title.

Earnest money   See Deposit.

Easement   The right a property owner has to use the land of another for a special purpose. It may be valid even if unidentified, unlocated, unmentioned, and unrecorded.

Emancipated minor   A person who is under the age to legally be an adult in the state in which they live but who has some other criteria that allow them to function as adults. The criteria may include being lawfully married or divorced, on duty in the armed forces, or emancipated by court order.

Eminent domain   Governments' power that allows them to take private property for public use after paying what they feel to be a fair price.

Encumbrance   A charge, claim, or lien against a property or personal right or interest in a property that affects or limits the title but does not prevent transfer.

Equity   The part of a property's current value that is owned and on which no money is owed; the property's value minus the liens owed against the property.

Escrow   A process in the transfer of real property in which buyers and sellers deposit documents or money with a neutral third party (the escrow holder). Buyers and sellers give instructions to the escrow holder to hold and deliver documents and money if certain conditions are met.

Escrow instructions   A written agreement between sellers and buyers that extrapolates the purchase contract into a form used as directions on how to conduct and close the escrow.

Exclusive agency listing   A listing with only one agency that provides that if the real estate professional obtains the buyer, you must pay the broker the commission. If you sell your home yourself, you are not liable for the commission.

Exclusive right to sell listing   A listing providing that, during the time listed, only that broker has the right to sell your home and earn the commission no matter who makes the sale.

Extended coverage title insurance   This coverage protects against numerous risks that are not a matter of record.

FHA   Federal Housing Administration; a federal governmental agency that manages FHA-insured loans to protect lenders in case of default by buyers.

FHA loan   Financing by having a conventional loan made by a lender and insured by the Federal Housing Administration.

Fiduciary   A person who is in a position of trust who must act in the best interest of clients.

Fire insurance   See Hazard insurance.

Fixed-rate loan   A loan on which the percentage of interest remains at the same rate over the life of the loan. The payments of principal remain equal during the entire period.

Fixture   Items permanently attached to or for which special openings were made in a home and its associated structures.

Fix-up costs   The expenses of improvements, repairs, and attractiveness items.

Flood Hazard Area Disclosure   A federally required disclosure to inform buyers that the property is located in a region designated as a special flood hazard area.

Flyers   Leaflets for mass distribution.

Foreclosure   The process by which a property on which a borrower has not paid is sold to satisfy a loan against the property.

Fraud   Willfully concealing or misrepresenting a material fact in order to influence another person to take action. The action results in the person's loss of property or legal rights.

FSBO   For sale by owner; a phrase describing a homeowner selling property without using a real estate broker.

Geological inspection   Inspection for potential or actual geological problems, as well as examination of records to determine whether property falls within any special zones.

Gift deed   A deed given for love and affection.

GI loan   See VA loan.

Grant deed   A deed using the word grant in the clause that transfers ownership.

Grantee   Buyer; receiver of a title to a property.

Grantor   Seller; holder of a title to a property.

Gross income   Total income it is possible to receive before operating expenses.

Guarantee of title   A warranty that title is vested in the party shown on the deed.

Hazard insurance   Casualty insurance, fire insurance; insurance protection against stated specific hazards such as fire, hail, windstorms, earthquakes, floods, civil disturbances, explosions, riots, theft, and vandalism.

Home equity line of credit   Credit given by a lender based on the amount of one's equity in a property. The line of credit becomes a loan secured by a mortgage or trust deed when the borrower uses some or all of the credit.

Home inspection   See Physical inspection.

Home inspector   A qualified person who examines and reports on the general condition of a home's site and structures.

Homeowner's association dues   Monthly fees owners of homes pay to their homeowner's association for the items it provides.

Homeowner's insurance   A policy protecting a homeowner from liability and casualty hazards listed in the policy. (See also Hazard insurance.)

Home protection plan   See Home warranty.

Home warranty   Home protection plan; insurance that items listed are in working order for the specified length of time.

Impounds   Reserve fund; funds held by the lender to assure payment in the future of recurring expenses. These expenses can include insurance premiums and taxes.

Improper delivery   Delivery of a deed that has not passed out of seller's control and/or was not delivered to buyers during the seller's lifetime.

Improvement costs   Expenses for permanent additions.

Improvement notices   Documents sent by governments giving notice of one-time charges for planned improvements (e.g., sidewalks).

Imputed interest rate   The minimum rate the IRS requires for a seller-financed loan. If you charge less than the minimum rate, the IRS taxes you on the minimum.

Index   A measurement of interest rates on which changes in interest charges on adjustable rate loans are based.

Inspection records   Notices indicating that inspections have been conducted by the proper local authorities at certain specified points in the building process.

Inspection reports   Reports by inspectors about the condition of various aspects of your property, including defects and repairs considered necessary.

Installment note   A loan paid back in at least two payments of principal on different dates.

Installment sale   A sale that allows the seller to receive payments in more than one tax year.

Interest   A charge or rate paid in arrears (after incurred) to a lender for borrowing money.

Interest-only loan   A loan for which only the interest is paid and no principal is repaid until the final installment.

Interpleader action   Request by a closing agent or escrow holder that a court take custody of the deposited funds and make a judgment as to their distribution.

Jointly and severally liable   Liable along with other parties and per-sonally liable.

Joint tenancy   Vesting wherein two or more parties acquire title at the same time. Each party has an equal, undivided interest and equal right to possess the property, including automatic right of survivorship.

Judgment   Final determination by a court of a matter presented to it. A general monetary obligation on all property of the person who owes the money. This obligation applies in each county where an abstract of the court judgment was recorded.

Kick-out provision   See Contingency release.

Lack of capacity   Inability to enter into a contract because one is not a competent person by his or her state's criteria.

Landfill   Soil moved onto the site from another location.

Landlord   The owner or lessor of real property.

Land sales contract   Contract for deed, real property sales contract; an agreement in which the seller retains title to property until the buyer performs all contract conditions.

Lease   A contract that transfers possession and use of designated property for a limited, stated time under specified conditions.

Lease option   A contract that stipulates that potential buyers are leasing a property for an agreed-on rental payment. These buyers have the right to purchase the property before the specified future date for the amount listed in the contract. Part of the lease payment is considered option money toward the purchase price.

Lease purchase   A contract that states that buyers are leasing the property for the agreed-on amount and conditions. The buyers agree to purchase the property at the agreed-on time for the agreed-on amount.

Legal description   A formal description giving a property's location, size, and boundaries in written and/or map form.

Lessee   The tenant or person who leases property from the landlord in order to use it.

Lessor   The landlord or owner of property who leases the property to the tenant for the tenant's use.

Liability   Responsibility for damages to other people or property; what you owe against an asset.

Lien   A claim against a property making the property security for debts such as loans, mechanic's liens, and taxes.

Lien releases   Documents releasing one from monetary liability to the party listed after fully paying that party.

Liquidated damages   The amount of money you may keep if the buyers default or breach the contact.

Lis pendens   An official recorded notice that legal action is pending against the title to the property.

Listing   Authorization to sell; a contract allowing a real estate broker to act as an agent to buy, lease, or sell property for another.

Litigation   Lawsuits.

Loan disclosure statement   A lender's account summary required by the Federal Truth in Lending Act.

Loan discount fee   See Points.

Loan fees   One-time charges by the lender for initiating a loan, including points, appraisal, and credit report on buyers.

Loan origination fee   Lender's charge for arranging and processing a loan, usually based on a percentage of the loan.

Loan tie-in fee   A fee charged by whoever handles closing for their work and liability in conforming to the lender's criteria for the buyer's new loan.

Market value   The amount buyers are willing to pay and sellers are willing to accept within a reasonable time.

Marshal's deed   See Sheriff's deed.

Material facts   Any facts that if known would influence a person's decision.

Mechanic's lien   A claim filed against property by a contractor, service provider, or supplier for work done or materials provided for which full payment has not been received.

Median price   The price at which half the properties are more expensive and half the properties are less expensive.

MLS   See Multiple Listing Service.

Mortgage   A contract to secure a loan by which you promise your property without giving up possession or title.

Mortgage default insurance   Default insurance; insurance coverage enabling the lender to receive a part of the outstanding balance in the event you default.

Mortgage disability insurance   Insurance coverage enabling you to pay monthly mortgage charges in the event you are totally and permanently disabled.

Mortgagee   Lender of money on property using a mortgage.

Mortgage life insurance   Insurance coverage enabling whomever you designate to pay the loan balance if you die.

Mortgagor   Property owner who borrows money using a mortgage.

Multiple Listing Service   MLS; an agency to which real estate brokers belong in order to pool their listings with other real estate brokers. If a sale is made, the listing and selling brokers share the commission.

Negative amortization   Process in which payments on a loan do not cover interest payments and the difference between the payment and interest due are added to the loan balance.

Net listing   A listing providing that the broker retain all money received in excess of the price set by the seller.

Net operating income   NOI; gross income minus operating expenses.

Nominal interest rate   Interest rate stated in a promissory note.

Nonconforming uses   Preexisting uses of land allowed to continue even though a current ordinance excluding that use has been enacted for that area.

Notary fee   A charge paid to a notary public to witness signatures on some of the legal documents in a transaction.

Notice of default   Warning sent to a borrower on a loan cautioning the borrower that the payment is delinquent.

Offset statement   A statement regarding a loan provided by the seller when a beneficiary statement is not available.

Open listing   A nonexclusive right-to-sell agreement one can make with one or more real estate professionals. It provides that if you sell your home yourself, you are not liable to the broker for a commission. If, however, a real estate professional obtains the buyers for the property, you must pay the broker the commission you have negotiated.

Operating expenses   Property taxes, insurance, maintenance, and utilities.

Option   A contract to keep an offer to buy, sell, or lease property open for a period and under the agreed-on terms.

Optionee   The person who gets the option on a property.

Optionor   The owner of a title who gives an option.

Option to buy   See Purchase option.

Payment records   Checks, receipts, and written ledgers.

Payment statements   Monthly stubs showing your payment date, amounts applied to principal and interest, and remaining balance due, as well as annual summary statements.

Permission-to-show listing   A listing contract that allows a real estate professional to show your property only to the person or persons named in that contract. You pay the commission only if someone on the list purchases your home.

Personal property   Items that are not permanently attached to your home or other structures on your property.

Pest control inspection   Structural pest control inspection, termite inspection; inspection for infestation or infection by wood-destroying pests or organisms.

Physical inspection   Home inspection; examination of the general physical condition of a property's site and structures.

Planned unit development   PUD; a subdivision in which the lots are separately owned but other areas are owned in common.

Points   Discount points, loan discount fee; a one-time charge by the lender to adjust the yield on the loan to current market conditions or to adjust the rate on the loan to market rate. Each point is equal to 1 percent of the loan balance.

Power of attorney   A document that gives one person the power to sign documents for another person.

Power of sale clause   A provision in a loan allowing the lender to foreclose and sell borrower's property publicly without a court procedure.

Preliminary title report   Report summarizing the title search performed by a title company or lawyer for a property.

Prepayment penalty   A fine imposed on a borrower by a lender for the early payoff of a loan or any substantial part of a loan.

Principal   One of the parties in a real estate transaction, either the sellers or the buyers.

Principal residence   An IRS term denoting the residence wherein you spend the most time during the tax year.

Probate court   A court that handles wills and the administration of estates of people who have died.

Promissory note   The written contract you sign promising to pay a definite amount of money by a definite future date.

Property taxes   Taxes; taxes assessed on property at a uniform rate so that the amount of the tax depends on the value.

Property tax statements   Documents that the county assessor's office mails to homeowners itemizing the semiannual or annual tax bill on a home and indicating the payment due dates.

Prorations   Proportional distributions of responsibility for the payment of the expenses of homeownership. This distribution is based on the percentage of an assessment or billing period during which the seller and buyers own the property.

PUD   See Planned unit development.

Purchase contract   The contract containing terms and conditions to which you and the buyers agree when you accept the buyers' offer to purchase your home.

Purchase option   Option to buy; the type of contract in which buyers agree to purchase the property for the amount listed in the contract, if they decide to buy your home and make the purchase within the listed period of time, and agree that you keep the option fee if they do not buy the property.

Quitclaim deed   A deed using the word quitclaim in the clause granting ownership and thus releasing the grantor from any claim to that property. A quitclaim deed has no warranties.

Real estate   See Real property.

Real estate broker   A real estate agent who represents another person in dealing with third parties. This person must take required courses, pass a broker's exam, and be state licensed. A broker may employ other qualified individuals and is responsible for their actions.

Real estate professional   A real estate broker or sales associate.

Real estate sales agent   A person who is licensed by a state and who represents a real estate broker in transactions.

Real Estate Settlement Procedures Act   See RESPA.

Real property   Real estate; land and whatever is built on, growing on, or attached to the land.

Real property sales contract   See Land sales contract.

Reconveyance deed   A deed that records full satisfaction of a trust deed-secured debt on your property and transfers bare legal title from the trustee to you.

Recording   Official entry of liens, reconveyances, and transactions into the permanent records of a county.

Release of contract   An agreement that all responsibilities and rights occurring as a result of a contract are invalid.

Repair costs   Expenses for work maintaining a home's condition, including replacement and restoration.

Request for notice of default   A recorded notice allowing a county recorder to notify lenders of foreclosure on a property in which the lender has an interest.

Rescind   To cancel a contract and restore the parties to the state they would have been in had the contract never been made.

Reserve fund   See Impounds.

RESPA   Real Estate Settlement Procedures Act; a federal law that requires that buyers be given, in advance of closing, information regarding their loan.

Restrictions   Encumbrances that limit the use of real estate by specifying actions the owner must take or cannot take on or with his or her property.

Revocation   Involuntary cancellation that occurs when the time limit has expired and one or both parties do not perform in accordance with the terms of the contract.

Sale leaseback   An agreement in which the seller sells the property to buyers who agree to lease the property back to the seller.

Sales associate   A real estate professional with either a broker's or sales license who acts as an agent for a broker.

Satisfaction of mortgage   A document indicating that you have paid off your mortgage in full.

Seller buy-down loan   A loan in which the effective interest rate is bought down (reduced) during the beginning years of the loan by contributions a seller makes.

Seller carry-back loan   A loan for which the seller acts as a lender to carry back or hold mortgage notes from buyers. These notes may be first, second, or even third loans.

Seller's agent   See Listing.

Seller's market   A condition in which there are more buyers than sellers; prices generally increase.

Selling agent   See Buyer's agent.

Setback   Laws prohibiting the erection of a building within a certain distance of the curb.

Settlement   See Closing.

Settling   Sinking and then coming to rest in one place.

Severalty   Vesting of title in which you hold title by yourself.

Sheriff's deed   Marshal's deed; a deed used by courts in foreclosure or in carrying out a judgment. This deed transfers a debtor's title to a buyer.

Short-sale provision   A lender reducing the amount of the loan payoff.

Single agent   An agent representing only one party in a real estate transaction.

Sliding   The large downward movement of a soil mass out of its previous position.

Slippage   The small downward movement of a soil mass out of its previous position.

Special endorsements   Specific endorsements that modify, expand, or delete the coverage of any insurance policy.

Special Studies Zone Disclosure   A form used to inform buyers that a property is in an area specified as a Special Studies Zone by California law. These zones primarily affect areas where there was or may be serious earthquake destruction.

Specific performance   Law that allows one party to sue another to perform as specified under the terms of their contract.

Standard coverage title insurance   The regular investigation for this insurance generally reveals only matters of record and location of the improvements with respect to the lot line.

Straight note   A promise to pay a loan in which the principal is paid as one lump sum, although the interest may be paid in one lump sum or in installments.

Structural pest control inspection   See Pest control inspection.

Subescrow fee   A fee charged by some escrow holders for their costs when they handle money.

Subject-to loan An existing loan for which buyers take over responsibility for the payments and seller remains primarily liable in the event of a deficiency judgment.

Survey fee A fee charged for a survey showing the exact location and boundaries of a property.

Syndication A form of limited partnership used to make real estate investments.

Take sheet A form used to collect information necessary to prepare the escrow instructions.

Tax deed Controller's deed; a deed used by a state to transfer title to the buyers.

Taxes See Property taxes.

Tax parcel number The number assigned to a piece of property by the local taxing authority.

Tax preparers Persons who prepare tax returns.

Tax stamps A method of denoting that a transfer tax has been paid in which stamps are affixed to a deed before the deed may be recorded.

Telephone register A listing of information regarding telephone calls you receive.

Termination of agency Ending of an agency agreement.

Termite inspection See Pest control inspection.

Time is of the essence A statement that one party in a contract must perform certain acts within the stated period before the other party can perform.

Title Evidence of one's right to a property and the extent of that right.

Title insurance The policy issued to you by the title company on completion of the final title search protecting against claims in the future based on circumstances in the past.

Title insurance companies Companies issuing title insurance policies.

Title search An examination of information recorded on your property at the county recorder's office. This examination verifies that the property has no outstanding claims or liens against it to adversely affect the buyer or lender and that you can transfer clear legal title to the property.

Transfer fee   See Assumption fee.

Transfer tax   Documentary transfer tax; a tax that some states allow individual counties or cities to place on the transferring of real property.

Trust deed   A document, used as a security device for the loan on your property, by which you transfer bare (naked) legal title with the power of sale to a trustee. This transfer is in effect until you have totally paid off the loan.

Trustee   A person who holds bare legal title to a property without being the actual owner of the property. The trustee has the power of sale for the lender's benefit.

Trustee's deed   A deed used by a trustee in a foreclosure handled outside of court to transfer the debtor's title to buyers.

Trust funds   Funds held by a closing agent or escrow holder for the benefit of the buyers or seller.

Truth in lending   A federal law that requires disclosure of loan terms to a borrower who is using his or her principal residence as security for a loan.

Unconditional lien release   Waiver of liens; a release, usually signed by a contractor, after a job is complete and you made the final payments waiving and releasing all rights and claims against your home.

Unenforceable   Not able to be enforced; void.

Unlawful detainer   The unjustifiable keeping of possession of real property by someone who originally had the right to possession but no longer has that right.

Unmarketability of title   Inability to sell property because of unacceptable encumbrances and liens on the title.

Usury   Interest charged in excess of what state law permits.

VA   Veterans Administration; the federal government agency that manages VA loans.

VA loan   GI loan; financing made by having a conventional loan made by a lender guaranteed by the Veterans Administration.

Variance   An approved release from current zoning regulations regarding the use or alteration of property.

Vendee   Purchaser or buyer.

Vendor   Owner or seller.

Vesting   Interest that cannot be revoked.

Veterans Administration   See VA.

Void   To have no effect; unenforceable at law.

Voidable   Able to be set aside.

Waive   Unilateral voluntary relinquishment of a right of which one is aware.

Waiver of liens   See Unconditional lien release.

Walk-through inspection   Buyer's physical examination of a property within a few days before closing verifying that systems, appliances, and the house itself are in the agreed-on condition.

Warranties   Printed or written documents guaranteeing the condition of property or its components.

Warranty deed   A deed in which the grantor explicitly guarantees the title to be as indicated in the deed. The grantor agrees to protect buyers against all claimants to the property.

Wipeout clause   See Contingency release.

Work stoppage clause   A clause in a contract giving a contractor the right to stop work if you do not make the required payments.

Wraparound mortgage   See All-inclusive trust deed.

Yield The return on investment including interest and principal expressed annually.

Zoning   Governmental laws establishing building codes and governing the specific uses of land and buildings.

INDEX